BENEDICT RULES – OK!

DAILY READING OF THE RULE OF SAINT BENEDICT FOR YOUNG PEOPLE

Vena Eastwood

GRACEWING

First published in 2001
as *Benedict Rules* by Source Books,
Trabuco Canyon, California

First published in England in 2007 by
Gracewing
2 Southern Avenue, Leominster
Herefordshire, HR6 0QF

ISBN 0 85244 680 2
ISBN 978 0 85244 680 5

Printed in England

To my mother,
Elizabeth 'Lizzie' Eastwood,
whose Benedictine hospitality was unknown to her
but experienced by many.

ACKNOWLEDGMENTS

Thank you –to Holy Father Benedict of Nursia, that master of community and spiritual giant who reaches from the sixth century into and beyond this new millennium. He has changed many lives and many communities, including my own. –To Esther de Waal and to Joan Chittister o.s.b., both of whose writings have been an inspiration and whose friendship has been a great encouragement. –To the Benedictine Sisters of Erie, Pennsylvania, whose unique charism, friendship, hospitality and encouragement have been an inspiration, not only in this work, but also in my own spiritual growth. –To the Benedictine communities in England of West Malling, Stanbrook and Ampleforth. –And to Abbot Timothy Wright o.s.b., for his support and affirmation of my work in Chaplaincy.

Thank you –to the students and staff of Saint Benedict's School and Sixth Form Centre, Derby, where this work was first put into daily use.

Thank you —to Sister Mary Philip o.s.b., who was the first to read and correct my writing. –And to my many friends who have contributed to this book in ways they may never realize.

Thank you –to Father Luke Dysinger o.s.b., and to Abbot Francis o.s.b., of Saint Andrew's Abbey, Valyermo, California, for permission to use extracts from *The Rule of St. Benedict Latin and English,* Source Books, 1996.

Thank you –to Denis Clarke for editing my work.

Thank you –to Christine Vladimiroff o.s.b., Prioress of the Benedictine Sisters of Erie, PA, for her encouraging foreword.

CONTENTS

Foreword by Christine Vladimiroff O.S.B. ⸺ ix

Author's Introduction ⸺ xi

The Prologue ⸺ 1

Chapter 1: The Various Kinds of Monks ⸺ 7

Chapter 2: The Abbot (The Person In Charge) ⸺ 8

Chapter 3: Calling the Brothers to Council ⸺ 12

Chapter 4: What are the Tools of Good Works? ⸺ 15

Chapter 5: Obedience ⸺ 23

Chapter 6: Silence ⸺ 26

Chapter 7: Humility ⸺ 29

Chapters 8–18: Details of Services and their Content ⸺ 49

Chapter 19: The Discipline of Chanting the Psalms ⸺ 51

Chapter 20: Reverence In Prayer ⸺ 54

Chapter 21: The Deans of the Community ⸺ 55

Chapter 23: Punishment ⸺ 56

Chapters 25–27: Serious Faults ⸺ 60

Chapters 28–30: More About Correction ⸺ 63

Chapter 31: The Cellarer ⸺ 66

Chapter 32: Tools and Goods ⸺ 70

Chapter 33: Private Ownership ⸺ 73

Chapter 34: Whether All Should Receive Necessary Things Equally ⸺ 75

Chapter 35: The Kitchen Servers ⸺ 77

Chapter 36: The Sick ⸺ 81

Chapter 37: The Aged and Children ⸺ 83

Chapter 38: The Reader For the Week ⸺ 84

Chapter 39: The Measure of Food ⸺ 87

Chapter 40: The Proper Amount of Drink ⸺ 89

Chapter 41: Meal Times ⸺ 92

Chapter 42: Silence After Compline ⸺ 94

Chapter 43: Those Who Arrive Late at the Work of God ⸺ 95

Chapter 44: The Excommunicated —————————— 97

Chapter 45: Faults in the Oratory ————————— 99

Chapter 46: Faults in Other Matters ———————— 100

Chapter 47: Announcing the Hours for the Work of God ———— 103

Chapter 48: Daily Manual Labor ————————— 104

Chapter 49: The Observance of Lent ———————— 108

Chapter 50: Being Away from the Community ————— 111

Chapter 51: Brothers Who Are Not Going Far Away ——— 112

Chapter 52: The Oratory of the Monastery —————— 113

Chapter 53: The Reception of Guests ———————— 115

Chapter 54: Letters and Gifts —————————— 119

Chapter 55: Clothing and Footwear ———————— 120

Chapter 56: The Abbot's Table —————————— 123

Chapter 57: Artisans —————————————— 124

Chapter 58: Receiving New Members ———————— 126

Chapter 59: Offering Noble and Poor Children ————— 128

Chapter 60: Priests Who Wish to Live in the Monastery ——— 131

Chapter 61: How Visiting Monks are Received ————— 132

Chapter 62: The Priests of the Monastery —————— 133

Chapter 63: Rank in the Community ———————— 134

Chapter 64: Appointing an Abbot ————————— 136

Chapter 65: The Prior of the Monastery —————— 140

Chapter 66: The Monastery Porters ———————— 141

Chapter 67: Brothers Sent on a Journey —————— 143

Chapter 68: If an Impossible Task is Commanded of a Brother 144

Chapter 69: Not Defending Another in the Monastery ——— 145

Chapter 70: That They May Not Presume to Strike One Another 146

Chapter 71: That They Should Obey One Another ———— 147

Chapter 72: The Zeal That Monks Ought to Have ———— 149

Chapter 73: All of Just Observance is Not Contained in This Rule 150

Lectio Divina in the School Community ———————— 153

FOREWORD

In adolescence a person emerges from within the child who has occupied the world thus far. It is at this juncture of life, in high school, that special attention must be given to fostering spirituality in the young.

Benedict Rules presents the basic Benedictine monastic charism as seeing life as a whole. Benedictine spirituality is a way of integrating and balancing the polarities of life. If lived well, the Benedictine approach can bring joy, personal fulfillment and a sense of deep peace. Each human being, no matter their age, seeks community and a way to commit the force of their person to something greater than their own life. This is the gift we must give the emerging adult.

Benedict Rules provides an opportunity to initiate the young person into an authentic spirituality that will give them both the experience of belonging and the opportunity for giving life meaning. That is no small task. The young person feels the pull of a rampant individualism in modern culture, and yet hears Benedict teach that the only competition should be trying to be the first to show love and respect for the others with whom they share life. In an increasingly mobile world, putting down roots is seen as archaic, but Benedict teaches a stability of heart that will only deepen as the pace of adult life quickens.

Benedict Rules captures the spirit of the Rule of Benedict. It is clear and direct as it helps the adult mentor the young person in a way of living in this world. The application of the key aspects of the Rule touches the real world in which the student lives. The examples and exercises meet the student where they are in life. There is no avoiding a comparison with conventional wisdom which says that the accepted way of society is what makes life comfortable, and the wisdom of a fifteen hundred year-old Rule that presents a different but a well-worn path to holiness.

Benedict Rules is a unique contribution to the literature of spirituality. It has many applications and its approach will be effective with high school students and young adults. It does not teach prayer, it makes life a prayer.

Christine Vladimiroff o.s.b.
Prioress
Benedictine Sisters of Erie

INTRODUCTION

It would be difficult to count the many and varied translations and adaptations of the Rule of St. Benedict. Over the past fifteen hundred years there have been ample time and intellect applied to presenting the Rule to the needs of most people, although it is only recently that it has been taken up with enthusiasm and devotion by laity. The Rule has been increasingly at work in my life, and as a school teacher I have eventually come to feel that it could be adapted for young people, specifically young people in a school community.

My first encounter with the Rule came about twenty-five years ago when I would visit a Benedictine abbey for respite from the rigors of teaching physical education. Later, I visited another abbey as a retreatant, but my impression then was that the Rule applied only to monks and nuns and it was not directly part of my thinking or spiritual development.

My career changed course and I took a position as Deputy Head and teacher of religious education at another school. Administration and funding meetings did not fire me as much as the spiritual development of young people. Trying to interest youngsters in God on a Friday afternoon made me determined how to understand their inherent 'Godness,' and when the opportunity arose, I applied for work as the full-time Chaplain at Saint Benedict School in Derby, England.

Here, the Rule came to my rescue for the first time. The interviews for the job were gruelling and I felt that the expectations of the interviewers were such that only the Archangel Gabriel could have met them. As part of the process I was asked to give a presentation on 'Community.' I happened to be staying at the convent where I had once been a novice, and thinking over the presentation I was to make the next day, it seemed inadequate. I went to the library and there found a very musty Latin/English edition of the Rule of St. Benedict. I scanned the index for inspiration, and there it was in Chapter 68: 'When a Brother is Given an Impossible Task.' Thank you, Benedict!

I got the job, but despite now being in St. Benedict School and despite having used his Rule to great effect, I never thought to look at it again until two years later when, at a national meeting of chaplains, we were discussing how the lives of Saints, to whom most of our Catholic schools are dedicated, could be sources of inspiration. I found two translations of the Rule: Esther de Waal's *A Life Giving Way*, and Joan Chittister's *The Rule of Benedict, Insights for the Ages*. Both have been invaluable to me in this work, and also in my personal spiritual journey. The encouragement of these two well-known writers has spurred me to complete this simple adaptation.

However, though the adaptation may be simple, for 'novices' in schools, the Rule itself is dangerous. It has been suggested that it should carry a health warning! For, Saint Benedict and his Rule change lives today as surely as they did at the monastery of Monte Cassino in the sixth century.

I offered my school community the challenge of the Rule, and then as a member, not a leader, of that community found myself travelling to see the Rule at work elsewhere. I went to Monte Cassino, five times to Erie, Pennsylvania, to meet Sister Joan Chittister and to live and work alongside the sisters there, and to Chile to meet members of a lay Benedictine community called the Manquehue Movement. There I saw schools where the Rule and *Lectio Divina* are lived by staff and students daily, which results in all the benefits of a rich Benedictine spirituality.

Lectio Divina is a time-honored way of reading Scripture, practiced by Benedict and his monks and practiced today in religious and lay communities. You may wish to consider it for your community, as it may be considered an integral part of following the Rule. Notes and two examples of how Lectio can be conducted in a group are appended at the end of this book.

The Rule of St. Benedict in a School Community

I am convinced that St. Benedict can change your life and the life of your school community as his Rule brings Gospel values to the fore and helps the community and the individual to 'live lives worthy of our calling.' As teachers, the question we need to ask at the outset is: Do we have God's school with us in it, or do we have our school with God in it? If it is the latter, things will happen when the Rule of Saint Benedict is lived daily.

What can Benedict's Rule offer a school community in the twenty-first century? It can offer wisdom that leads to God, it can offer guidance in every situation found in a community and it can offer the context for solutions to the most prosaic problems. The Rule was written by a man whom, when young, became disillusioned by the degenerate world about him. As such, it speaks with compassion and understanding to young people who seek guidance in confusion and who are anxious for answers.

At the beginning of each section of a chapter, most editions of the Rule have three dates which facilitate the daily reading of the whole Rule three times a year. Thus, someone who has been a Benedictine monk or nun for fifty years will have read through the Rule one hundred and fifty times. One elderly nun wrote to me saying: "As one who has spent over half my life living the Rule of Benedict, I find it a fount of wisdom that never runs dry." Though school life is not structured like the monastic day, there is time in every schedule for prayer, tutorial time, or sharing of one sort or another. This adaptation of the Rule is simply presented so that it can be used as a whole school project, as a classroom meditation, perhaps for Morning Prayer, or as Assembly material. It can be used as part of a Religious Education program, at the beginning of lessons, developed as part of drama classes, or as a basis for small group discussions. Homeschoolers will find this adaptation invaluable.

Using This Adaptation

The Rule is not given here in its entirety—there are plenty of editions and commentaries available for those who wish to delve deeper. I have attempted to include enough passages to give a full flavor of the riches that can be found in the entire Rule. In three cases I have combined several chapters for consideration as one, because they go into such detail about a particular point that their classroom discussion would become repetitious. There are also two chapters which have not been included, 22 and 24, they deal with sleeping arrangements and 'The Degrees of Excommunication,' the applications of which are superfluous in a school.

Fr. Luke Dysinger's translation of the Rule, used here, is a recent one. It is an attempt to present very closely in English the phrases and cadences as St. Benedict wrote them, rather than as groups of Benedictines have adapted them for particular monasteries and convents over the years. Sometimes words may appear unnecessarily archaic, and there is no attempt at using words that are not gender specific. Teachers may forestall objections on these grounds by emphasizing that the Rule *is* ancient, a document that dates back to the end of the Western Roman Empire, and that it was addressed specifically to communities of men.

There is enough material on each page to form the basis of a complete class period. As necessary, if little time is devoted to discussion, any segment can be completed in fifteen minutes and it will still be beneficial. Though St. Benedict's chapters progress fairly naturally, it is not essential that they be taken in order. For instance, at the beginning of the school year it would be a good idea to take a look at Chapter 58, about receiving new members to the community.

Each segment consists of a quotation from the Rule, a paragraph for discussion—suggestions only—for the class, led by the teacher, and the whole is completed by prayer. Where necessary for the sake of clarity, I have made some introductory remarks at the beginning of chapters. Most importantly, following the prayer on many pages, there is a small section called either 'Challenge' or 'Food for Thought.' This is to emphasize to students that they are to take something away with them from their time with the Rule and use it in developing their own and the community's spirituality— to *live* the Rule rather than simply read it. These challenges and thoughts can be used at the leader's discretion, but often something arises in the students' discussion from which the leader can propose an appropriate action.

As with the Gospel, in which the Rule is steeped, the Rule can be dangerous stuff when people start to live it. Do not be surprised if St. Benedict sets the proverbial cat among the pigeons. Do not be discouraged if your community's spirituality develops in disorder. It has all happened before, this path that you have chosen, which started in Subiaco some fifteen hundred years ago, is well-trodden and it leads to God.

Listen, O my child, to the precepts of the master,
and incline the ear of your heart:
willingly receive and faithfully fulfill the admonition
of your loving father... (Prologue)

BENEDICT RULES

THE PROLOGUE

Introduction

The Prologue is a summary of the whole Rule of St. Benedict and gives a flavor of what it is all about. It also warns you not to proceed if you do not like the flavor of what you taste, because it could upset more than your stomach! The life-giving, life-changing Rule begins with a word that teachers use very often in their careers.

Prologue Section

Listen, O my child, to the precepts of the master, and incline the ear of your heart: willingly receive and faithfully fulfill the admonition of your loving father. (Prol. 1)

Discussion

–Sensible advice at the beginning of a new school year! Everyone has to listen to someone: teachers to the principal, pupils to their teacher, janitors to the caretaker, cooks to their supervisors, secretaries to their office managers, and so on. We need to listen, to learn and to understand. We need to listen to those who know. Once instructed, Benedict does not say just, "Get on with it," he tells us to carry out our instructions enthusiastically.

Prayer

Heavenly Father,
help us to listen to those who can help us,
and also to those we perhaps would prefer
not to listen to, but know we should.
Above all help us to listen to your still, small voice
which speaks to us at all times and in all places
if only we listen.
Amen.

Prologue Section

To you, therefore, my words are now addressed, whoever you are, that through renouncing your own will you may fight for the Lord Christ, the true king, by taking up the strong and bright weapons of obedience. (Prol. 3)

Discussion

Oh dear! Whoever we are, we have to listen to God and be obedient. Obedience is doing what we are told. That is difficult. It involves trusting those who give us the order, and responsibility to those who give it. Obedience is described as a strong and bright weapon, something which is good and which protects us. Let us use it.

Prayer

Jesus, you are God's Son,
but still you were obedient.
You did what was asked of you,
even to the point of a painful death.
Help us to be obedient, to do as we are asked.
And if we have to ask something of someone,
may we do it with respect and politeness
and in your love and strength.
Amen.

Prologue Section

First, whenever you begin any good work, beg of God with most earnest prayer to perfect it. (Prol. 4)

Discussion

This section forms part of A Prayer of St. Benedict. You will search for a long time to find something better to say at the beginning of any task—every piece of homework, every set of books to be corrected. The words are simple, brief and powerful. Write it out, learn it and use it. It will not do any harm, and it may do a lot of good! Worth a try for a better grade!

A Prayer of Saint Benedict

> We pray, Lord, that everything we do
> may be prompted by your inspiration
> so that every prayer and work of ours
> may begin from you
> and be brought by you to completion.
> Amen.

...A Shorter Version, or Arrow Prayer

> Jesus, we'll do anything you ask, but give us a hand!
> Amen.

Prologue Section

Let us then at last arise, since the Scripture arouses us saying, It is now time for us to rise from sleep. [ROMANS 13:11]. And let us open our eyes to the deifying light; let us attune our ears to what the divine voice admonishes us, daily crying out: Today if you hear his voice, harden not your hearts [PSALM 95:7-8]. (Prol. 8)

Discussion

We are being encouraged, urged to waken up to the fact that God is real and interested in everything we do and will help us if we listen and watch for God in our lives and work. Don't ignore it when you feel God guiding you. God is sound!

Prayer

Help us, Jesus, to wake up,
not only from our nightly rest,
but also from our sleepy faith.
Help us to see the joy and excitement in knowing you,
and to feel the security of knowing that
you love each one of us.
Amen.

Prologue Section

Hence also the Lord says in the Gospel: He who hears these words of mine and does them is like a wise man who built his house upon rock [MATTHEW 7:24]. (Prol. 33)

Discussion

When we get something new we often ask, "Is there a guarantee with it?" Here is our guarantee at the beginning of the Rule: If you follow the Rule, you will be like a sensible person. Listening is advised again. Let us look at this word 'Listen'. There are various reasons why we listen:

    a) to learn

    b) to help and comfort

    c) to teach

Do we do these things? Are we better at one than another?

Prayer

Lord Jesus, give us listening ears,
listening hearts and listening minds.
Help us to learn, to love and to instruct,
and to do these things in your strength
and with your love.
Amen.

Prologue Section

We have, therefore, to establish a school of the Lord's service. In instituting it we hope to establish nothing harsh or oppressive. ...Do not flee in dismay from the way of salvation which cannot be other than narrow at the beginning. (Prol. 45-46, 48)

Discussion

Come on—there is a reward and the kingdom of Christ's salvation on offer! The way to it is bound to be difficult, but we have a guide who is not harsh and hard, but full of love for us. Benedict uses the phrase, 'School of the Lord's service.' If ours were indeed the Lord's School what a place it would be to work and play in!

Prayer

Jesus, you never promised that following you
would be easy, soft or feeble.
We need your strength to help us to stick to the task
of building up your kingdom in this school,
so that it is no longer our school with you in it,
but your school with us in it.
Amen.

Challenge

There are forty-eight sections or verses in the Prologue. I have mentioned only a few. This is just a flavor of a flavor! Are you prepared to go on?

CHAPTER 1: THE VARIOUS KINDS OF MONKS

Chapter Section

There are four kinds of monks. First are the cenobites: that is, those who live in monasteries and serve under a rule and an abbot. The second kind are the anchorites, that is hermits...The third and most detestable kind are the sarabaites...whatever they think fit or choose to do, that they call holy. The fourth kind are the monks called gyrovagues...always wandering and never stable. (1:1, 3, 6, 10, 11)

Discussion

St. Benedict wants us to think about who we are. If we are students or teachers then probably we have not learned enough in life yet to come to God alone, outside a community, as the hermits try. If we are like the sarabites, then we are far too self-centered to care about anyone else in a community, we don't see the value in other people. If we are like the gyrovagues then we spend our time flitting from one idea or way of life to the next. We cannot settle long enough to be of benefit to other people or ourselves. But if we are like the cenobites then we understand how important a community and guidance are in serving God. St. Benedict has written his Rule for this kind of person.

Prayer

Jesus, you had a clear idea about who you were.
You knew the importance of the guidance
you had in the Word of God,
and you knew the importance of
the community of your disciples.
Help us to be like you.
Amen.

CHAPTER 2:
THE ABBOT (THE PERSON IN CHARGE)

Introduction

This chapter is about authority and how we each handle the authority we have been given, whether as head teacher, a member of staff, a staff associate, a pupil or a parent.

Chapter Section

An abbot who is worthy to govern a monastery must always remember what he is called and fulfill the name 'superior' in his deeds. For it is Christ's place that he is believed to hold in the monastery...(2:1, 2)

Discussion

Authority is a strange thing, enjoyed by some and suffered by others! With authority, power over others, comes the responsibility to use that power and authority properly. To make life difficult, or to use authority for selfish reasons is wrong, and St. Benedict disapproves of the wrong use of power. The Abbot must use his authority with careful thought and justice.

Prayer

Father, authority is a great responsibility.
It is something we need to be very careful with.
In greedy hands it can be destructive,
in responsible hands it can be creative.
We pray that whatever authority and power
over others we have been given,
we may use wisely and give you the glory.
Amen.

Chapter Section

The Abbot is not to distinguish between persons in the monastery. He should not love one more than another...
(2:16, 17)

Discussion

Whether we are teacher or pupil, we should not have favorites. We should not work better for one person than another, or harder in one lesson than another. Having favorites can lead to difficulties and makes people feel uncomfortable. We should try to work well for the good of everyone, said Benedict. Pause for thought: Do we have favorites? If so, is it really fair? Are we fair?

Prayer

Heavenly Father, we are often drawn
to certain people and certain things,
yet you show us that we are all loved equally by you
and are valuable in your eyes.
Help us to value one another and to treat others fairly.
Amen.

Chapter Section

And so, in obtaining by his admonitions the amendment of others, he will also amend his own vices. (2:40)

Discussion

Have you ever criticized someone and then found that you are doing the same thing of which you, yourself were critical? It is as though we are being taught a lesson: that we are all capable of mistakes and we should not be hard on others. We often learn very good lessons if we take on board our own criticism. 'You see a splinter in your brother's eye but do not notice the beam in your own' [MATTHEW 7:3].

Prayer

Jesus, may we have the humility to correct our own
faults and especially the ones that we are quick
to point out in others.
Amen.

Chapter Section

The abbot should never teach or enact or command anything that is contrary to the precepts of the Lord. (2:4)

Discussion

Schools do not have abbots but they do have people in charge, so the point is still relevant. Anyone who is put in charge has a duty to carry out their responsibilities in the way God would want them carried out. That is the fairest way and the best way. We have very high expectations of people in charge. We are only too ready to criticize when those in authority get something wrong—and even when they don't! How often do we pray for those with responsibility and who are under pressure? How often do we cause that pressure? So, let us pray...

Prayer

We pray for those in authority
and for those with responsibilities.
May they be guided by your example
so that they may lead wisely
both in what they say and what they do.
Amen.

CHAPTER 3:
CALLING THE BROTHERS TO COUNCIL

Introduction

This chapter is about consultation and listening to one another, as well as listening to the voice of God. 'O that today you would listen to his voice! Harden not your hearts...' [PSALM 95:7-8]. If God is trying to get through to you, don't shut off. It could be important!

Chapter Section

All should be called to council because it is often to the younger that the Lord reveals what is best. (3:3)

Discussion

We usually think that the voice of authority and experience—often the voice of the older members of a community—is right. Benedict, however, says that all should be listened to and all opinions should be valued. Sometimes the newcomer, or someone with a youthful, fresh approach comes up with an answer or at least a good suggestion. Everyone's suggestions having been considered, the person in charge should make the final decision, for the good of all.

Prayer

God, Our Father, help us always to make room
for the opinions of others.
Help each one of us, whatever position we hold,
to ask for your guidance in all that we do.
May what we decide be for the good of all.
Amen.

Chapter Section

Yet, even as it is natural for disciples to obey their master, so it is appropriate for him to settle everything with foresight and justice. (3:6)

Discussion

"It isn't fair!" How often do we hear or speak that phrase? Benedict tells us to be careful, to think things through until the wisest course is found. Then the person making a decision is as sure as he or she can be that it is fair. Letting God into our decision-making process is a certain way to get a fair outcome. But do we let God in?

Prayer

Father, if we put our hand in yours
and let you show us the way,
it may not be the easiest way, but it will be right.
Give us a feeling of security and faith
as we hand over important decisions to you.
Give us a sympathetic heart to enable us
to be aware of the feelings of others
and always to act with fairness.
Amen.

Chapter Section

In everything, therefore, all are to follow the Rule as their master: from it no one at all should have the temerity to turn aside. (3:7)

Discussion

This section may seem to contradict the last two, but it is telling us that if the previous two sections have been followed, the outcome should be fair and it should be followed. The informed majority decision should be accepted. As individuals, we may not always agree with a decision but we owe it to the community to follow what has been fairly decided.

Prayer

Jesus, there are times when things do not go our way.
There are situations which we find difficult
to make our own.
We ask for a spirit of acceptance
and an ability to see the other person's point of view.
Amen.

Food for Thought

'Do everything with counsel and you will not be sorry afterwards' [SIRACH 32:24].

CHAPTER 4:
WHAT ARE THE TOOLS OF GOOD WORKS?

Introduction

Speaking of high ideals is all very well, but it can lead people into confusion and feeling guilt when they find them difficult to achieve. In this chapter St. Benedict offers us very specific means to become close to God. Using these means will still be difficult, but we are not left floundering without direction.

Chapter Section

To become a stranger to worldly behavior; to prefer nothing to the love of Christ. To honor all. Not to store up wrath awaiting a time of revenge. Not to turn away from love. To bring forth the truth from heart and mouth. (4:20, 21, 23, 26, 28)

Discussion

Here are the basic tools for doing the job... And what is the job? —Living and behaving as Christians, people signed with the Sign of the Cross, paid up, active, loyal, hard-working members of Jesus' club. Are we using the tools? Are we doing the job?

Prayer

Father, you never ask us to do anything
without giving us the strength
and support to carry it out.
We ask that we will have the courage
to do the things you ask
and the sense to come to you for guidance.
Amen.

Chapter Section

Not to cause injury, but rather to bear it patiently. To love one's enemies. Not to curse those who curse you, but rather to bless them. (4:30-32)

Discussion

Good Heavens! You can't be serious! Yes, these are the words from the Gospels [Matthew 5:44, Luke 6:27-28], the teaching of Jesus, the teaching to which Benedict *always* points us. We may say this teaching is hard, and it is. But if we were to do all this, what an incredible difference it would make to the community! Why, then, does it not happen? It is difficult because we rely on our own strength to make it happen, but we need God for this difficult work. This chapter talks about the tools we are given to do these difficult things.

Prayer

God, this is difficult!
Help us to be the people that you want us to be.
Give us the strength not to follow the easy path.
We are sorry for the many times we let you,
each other and ourselves down.
Amen.

Chapter Section

To place your hope in God. To attribute whatever good you see in yourself to God, not to yourself; but always to clearly acknowledge and take personal responsibility for the wrongs you do. To fear the Day of Judgment: to dread hell. To daily keep death before your eyes. To keep custody at every hour over the actions of your life. To keep custody of your mouth against depraved speech. (4:41-45, 48, 51)

Discussion

Just when you think things are hard, they get harder! We feel like saying, "Get *real,* God!" But read the passage through again, slowly. The hardest thing is that it is right! What is this part about death? Well, we will have to give an account of what we have done, how we have lived, and above all, how we have loved. If we keep that in mind, guarding our mouths—not swearing, for instance—is easy.

Prayer

God, it seems you ask too much of us!
But on the other hand, You don't say,
"Do this, and I'll help you,"
You say, "I'll help you, and you'll do it!"
God, help us!
Amen.

Chapter Section

To listen willingly to holy readings, to prostrate frequently in prayer. (4:55-56)

Discussion

Now, this seems easier. But do we do it? How often are we turned off by the thought of a reading from the Bible? Despite all its wisdom and guidance, we think it is uninteresting. Why not look at it again when you have a spare moment? The words of Jesus in Matthew 5:3-12 are a great place to get involved in a conversation with Jesus. Prayer is that time we spend with Jesus, whom we call Friend. If we spoke as little with our school friends as we do with Jesus, I don't think we would have many friends. Jesus, our much-neglected friend is always waiting for us just to be with Him. Jesus is interested in everything we do and say. Let's share it with him.

Prayer

God, people say, "It's good to talk!"
Help us to spend some time with you,
help us to talk and to listen.
We need you to be close to us, and you are,
but help us to be close to you in prayer.
Amen.

Chapter Section

Do not love quarrelling: flee from conceit, revere the elders and love the juniors. (4:68-71)

Discussion

This passage helps everyone survive in community life. We will sometimes argue and be angry with other people, and maybe with ourselves. But respecting and loving other people, being aware of their needs and letting them help us or listen to us, is an important part of living and working with others. Being friendly to everyone, no matter who they are or how much more or less important they are than you, is very worthwhile.

Prayer

Jesus, we ask for the gift of Patience.
Help us to be cheerful and friendly,
especially when we are with others.
We ask for your love in our hearts
as we listen to those who are troubled in any way.
Amen.

Chapter Section

Make peace with opponents before the setting of the sun. (4:73)

Discussion

Benedict's humanity shows here: he realizes we quarrel and fall out with one another. There are people in the school community who get on our nerves, cause difficulties. If we look into our God-given toolbox, we find an essential tool: Forgiveness. We do have broken relationships and we resist making peace. To do nothing to try to mend the relationship makes things worse. The longer the act of healing is left, the more difficult it becomes. So, before the day is over, try to mend the friendship with the tools of Forgiveness and Love.

Prayer

Jesus,
we ask that we will have the courage to say sorry,
especially for broken relationships and friendships.
We ask for your healing
so that we can accept our friends as you accept them.
Forgive us our trespasses
as we forgive those who trespass against us.
Amen.

Chapter Section

And never to despair of the mercy of God. (4:74)

Discussion

We will have many problems to tackle in our school lives. God knows we are going to struggle at times but He does not expect us to struggle through alone. He will always be there to give us a hand, so we will never have to take on the burdens of a problem in full. After all, a problem shared is a problem halved. Shared with God, it may very well disappear!

Prayer

God, we give you thanks
for your constant presence in our lives.
We ask that you will keep us
mindful of that presence.
Amen.

Chapter Section

The workshop in which we diligently use all these tools is the enclosure of the monastery and stability in the community. (4:78)

Discussion

Our workshop is school. The tools to be used are one day to be handed back to the Giver, God, and we will give account for the condition of the tools. Have we used the tool of Forgiveness well and often? Have we used the tools of Prayer, of Listening, of Reading God's Word, and above all, the tool of Love? We will not be asked if we have reached the tops of our professions, whether we have gained vast numbers of certificates or made lots of money. We will be asked how well and how much we used the best tool of all, *Love*.

Prayer

May the Love of God,
seen in the generous Love of Jesus
and the gift of Love of the Holy Spirit,
fill our hearts, minds and our community,
today and always.
Amen.

Food for Thought

Is this God's school with us in it, or is it our school with God in it?

CHAPTER 5: OBEDIENCE

Introduction

This chapter is a tough one: it is about bending our will to someone else's. Not only does it suggest doing what we are told, but we have to do it willingly. We do it because we love, not for reward. This does work. The Rule has to be *lived,* not just read, and that can be tough, but that is no reason not to try. In trying we might surprise ourselves and others.

Chapter Section

The first step of humility is obedience without hesitation.
...as soon as anything is ordered by the superior. (5:1,4)

Discussion

To do as we are told is hard when we have to do something we do not like. If someone were to tell us to eat chocolate, we would probably say, "No problem!" But if we are told to get on with our work, to wash the dishes after dinner, to apologize, to pick up litter, to do homework—each of these is more of a problem than eating chocolate. Everyone has to take orders from someone at some time. Benedict says that we must quickly obey those set over us as though their orders come from God. Whether we like to or not is not an issue!

Prayer

Jesus, it is difficult to take orders,
especially if the task is unpleasant.
Help us to look at your obedience,
even to death on a cross.
May your death show us
how much you were prepared to give, and then,
perhaps, our task may not seem so difficult.
Amen.

Chapter Section

Such people, therefore, leaving immediately all that is theirs and forsaking their own wills, at once disengage their hands, and leaving unfinished what they were doing, follow by their deeds with the eager step of obedience, the voice of him who commands. (5:7, 8)

Discussion

If we are going to be obedient and follow the instructions that teachers give us, or if as teachers we are to follow the instructions of our managers, then we must carry them out wholeheartedly. We should stay on task and do the very best we can.

Prayer

Jesus, hurtful things were said to you.
Help us to cope with those
who say and do hurtful things.
Help us to 'go for it,'
when we know the task to be right.
Amen.

Chapter Section

If a disciple obeys with ill will, and murmurs [grumbles] not only with his lips but in his heart, even if he fulfills the command, he will not be acceptable to God... (5:17, 18)

Discussion

When God asks, not only are we to do the task, we are to do it in the right spirit, without grumbling aloud or in our minds. This is tough and demanding, but who said being a Christian is easy? Being a Christian in the way that St. Benedict calls for seems even more demanding! But with big demands come big rewards—eventually. Don't ask *when*. That is up to God.

Prayer

Lord, help us not to grumble
but to do what we are asked—willingly!
Amen.

Challenge

Now is a good time to put the Rule into practice. Start with something simple: for one day this week, when you are asked to do something unpleasant, do it with a smile—and immediately. Test your obedience. If we were all to act in this way, our school would grow in the values of the Gospel.

For instance: St. Benedict did not have soda cans and plastic wrappers to deal with so there is nothing in his Rule about litter, but he was very concerned about caring for the things that we have been given. So, look after creation, pick up the trash and put it where it belongs.

And if we don't want to take up this challenge, let us ask ourselves *Why not?*

CHAPTER 6: SILENCE

Chapter Section

But as for ridiculing or otiose words, which induce laughter, we permanently ban them in every place. (6:8)

Discussion

There are people in any school who spend a lot of time gossiping. Gossiping is one of the most damaging things you can do with words. Even if you are sure the gossip is true, is it any of your business? Would the person you are talking about be hurt if they could hear you? Benedict puts a total ban on gossip. Strong stuff! But, like acid, gossip is corrosive and it destroys a community.

Prayer

Jesus, the gift of speech is given by you.
May we always treasure it and use it for good
and not for hurting others.
Give us courage not to have anything to do with gossip.
It is so easy to join in.
Amen.

Chapter Section

...if we ought to refrain even from good words for the sake of restraining speech, how much more ought we to abstain from evil words, on account of the punishment due to sin! (6:2)

Discussion

For the sake of silence, it is better at times not even to say good things! This may seem strange at first because probably we all feel more comfortable with conversation than silence. Benedict is not talking about silence as just avoiding noise, but rather as a deep, inner silence where we can meet and be with God. It has been said that the deepest prayer does not involve words. This type of prayer is called Contemplation. Anyone can try it! In class it is wrong to talk when we are supposed to be quiet, even if what we say is good. So, in this case, obedience and silence go hand in hand.

Prayer

Lord, we live in a world of noise and commotion.
We ask that we may learn to appreciate that
silence is not just an absence of noise
but a place where we can meet you.
Amen.

Chapter Section

Speaking and teaching befit the master: remaining silent and listening are proper for the disciple. (6:6)

Discussion

Benedict is again encouraging us to listen. Firstly to God and to see God represented to us in our superiors. They may be our class teacher, abbot, novice guardian, tutor, line manager, head teacher or parent. We must also remember that when we are in the position of a superior, we have a responsibility to those whom we teach and direct.

Prayer

Father, we ask that
we may use our responsibility wisely,
that those who look to us for help,
guidance and direction
may hear your will in our requests.
Amen.

CHAPTER 7: HUMILITY

Introduction

To say this chapter is tough is an understatement. As always, Benedict is strict, but at the same time encouraging and understanding of our weaknesses. This understanding is a challenge to us to strive towards becoming what God wants us to be. Benedict describes twelve steps to achieving humility.

Chapter Section

Holy Scripture cries out to us saying: Everyone who exalts himself shall be humbled and he who humbles himself shall be exalted [LUKE 14:11]. (7:1)

Discussion

In her book, *The Rule of St. Benedict, Insight for the Ages,* Joan Chittister o.s.b. makes us realize how important humility is if we are to live correctly: "When we make ourselves God, no one is safe in our presence." Humility is at times confused with humiliation. To humiliate someone reflects on the person doing the humiliating. To belittle another is vile. But to seek humility in ourselves is pleasing to God. Consider these two dialogues:

Example 1: "You! Yes, you, stupid! Pick up that box and put it over there—yes, *there,* you idiot!"

"Who do you think you're talking to? Don't call me an idiot! Pick up your own lousy box!"

Example 2: "You! Yes, you, stupid! Pick up that box and put it over there—yes, *there,* you idiot!"

"Yes, okay. Over here. Is that right?" [Said without sarcasm].

Example two is the one that shows humility. The way
the first person spoke is not the problem of the second,
it is the first person's problem. Yes, it is hard and
unusual to react as in example two, but if we want to
change our community and ourselves, we may have to
change the habits of a lifetime.

Prayer

God, give us the help and strength
and understanding to be humble.
To be humble is very difficult,
but it will change us and our community
if we keep trying.
Help us never to make anyone look small or
uncomfortable with our words and actions.
Amen.

Chapter Section (Step 1)

The first step of humility, then, is that one always keeps 'the fear of God before his eyes' [PSALM 36:2]... Let us consider that we are regarded from heaven by God at every hour. (7:10, 13)

Discussion

Would we do all that we do if we really believed God was watching us? Sometimes we do not do things if we know our parents or teachers are watching. God really does see all that we do! Yet he sees us with love, forgiveness and reconciliation. That should encourage us to act properly and in His strength. We need to recognize that God is God.

Prayer

Help us to believe in you,
and to believe that you are God.
You know what is best for us in every situation.
You see us always and everywhere,
and because you love us,
you will do what is best for us.
Amen.

Chapter Section (Step 1)

And so to we request of God in the prayer that His will may be done in us [MATTHEW 6:10]. (7:20)

Discussion

Benedict quotes frequently from the Scriptures. His life is steeped in the Psalms and the Gospels. How steeped in Scripture are you? Do you have a Bible? Do you read the Bible at home or at school for pleasure or guidance, or do you use it only in RE class? It is said that the Bible is the greatest gift this world affords, that it has all the answers, comfort and guidance we need. It is God's Word, the Good News. But where is it in our lives? Why not read a couple of verses each day and think about them? Since we are talking about humility at the moment, reading Isaiah 2:9 and Philippians 2:8, would be useful. —Anyone got a Bible handy?

Prayer

God, you have given us Scriptures.
Help us to read, learn and remember them
so that they may have an affect on our lives
and the life of this community.
Amen.

Challenge

Bite your tongue when someone tries to make you look small. Rise above your hurt pride and you will be a giant!

Chapter Section (Step 1 continued)

And so to we request of God in the prayer that His will may be done in us. (7:21)

Discussion

Benedict suggests that if we are persistent we will get an answer to our prayers, but we must accept that God's will may be different from ours. Striving for perfection is not what gets us to God, rather it is our persistence, our not giving up or turning away from a challenge. It is a slog, but worth it!

Prayers

Our Father who art in heaven...
So often we pray the prayer that you gave us,
but often we don't think about the words.
Help us today to pray for what you want to happen.
Amen.

•

Lord, help us to make the right decisions
even if it means losing popularity
and our reputation.
Amen.

Chapter Section (Step 2)

The second step of humility is that one does not love his own will...(7:31)

Discussion

We need to try to put God at the center of all that we do. When we are asked to do something, we do it without question: "Go to the back of the line," or, "Pick up that trash." No questions asked, just do it. No "I was here first," or "I didn't drop it." How many times today have you said "No" when you have been asked to do something? With God at the center, these tasks are unimportant and just need doing. We should remember that God's will is best.

Prayer

Jesus,
you spent a tough time in the Garden of Gethsemane,
asking God to take your suffering away.
But you took the task given to you
and went to the cross.
Help us to put our self-interest to one side
and to do what is asked of us without question.
Amen.

Chapter Section (Step 3)

The third step of humility is that for the love of God one submits himself in all obedience to his superior, imitating the Lord, of whom the apostle says: He was made obedient even unto death [PHILIPPIANS 2:8]. (7:34)

Discussion

Obedience—even if it means missing out on something: our favorite lesson, our place in line, our time with friends. How often do we complain or disobey because of our personal wants? Benedict says that we should not worry about them, there is no great loss. Our instincts must be subject to doing what is right: for instance, we may have to walk away from a fight, lose face, be called 'chicken.' It is often hard to do God's will, but it is always right. We must always be ready to receive correction.

Prayers

For the times we think only about ourselves,
Lord, we are sorry,
and ask for strength to follow your example
of obedience,
even if it is costly.
Amen.

•

Jesus, help us to do what we have been asked
with a good attitude and in the right frame of mind.
Amen.

Chapter Section (Step 4)

The fourth step of humility is that if in the exercise of this very obedience hard and contrary things, even injustices, are done to one, he embraces patience silently in his conscience, and in enduring does not weaken or give up, as Scripture says: he who perseveres to the end will be saved [MATTHEW 10:22]. (7:35-36)

Discussion

As if the previous steps were not hard enough! Now we have the situation where through misunderstanding we get unfair treatment. We need to keep asking ourselves, "What would God want me to do?" And, "How would God want me to react?"

Prayer

Lord, it is hard to work for others,
especially when it may lead us to being misunderstood.
Help us to accept the things that are difficult
because they are what enable us to grow.
Amen.

Challenges

• Don't answer back when told to do something you object to.

• Ask God what to do in any situation where you need advice.

• Try saying to God, "Over to you. I don't want to go it alone, you know what is best."

Food For Thought

God is in the dregs of our lives. That's why it takes humility to find God where God is not expected to be!
JOAN CHITTISTER O.S.B.

Chapter Section (Step 5)

Make known to the Lord your way and hope in Him [PSALM 37:5]. And again Scripture says: Confess to the Lord, for He is good [PSALM 106:1]. (7:45-46)

Discussion

This chapter about humility gets more and more difficult as it develops, but no matter how difficult it is, one has to admit that if we accomplished what Benedict teaches, it would change our school, our relationships, our work and our selves for the better. 'It is not in the reading but in the doing!'

Revealing the self, personal honesty is essential for growth, says Benedict. Owning up when we have done wrong is important, even when no one else sees that we have done wrong. We do not need to tell God, for God knows everything. We need to admit our wrong to ourselves as much as to others. For example, you kick a football and smash a window but nobody sees you do it. Do you think you can get away with it? Benedict says that you must own up so something can be done to correct the fault. If you do not admit your faults then you fool only yourself.

Prayer

Lord, when we do something that we know is wrong
but which goes unnoticed,
help us to come clean and admit it.
Father, help us to see that the truth
is always pleasing to you.
Amen.

Chapter Section (Step 6)

I was reduced to nothing and did not realize it; I have become like a beast before you, yet I am always with you [PSALM 73:22-23]. *(7:50)*

Discussion

Our society is all for getting and having, wanting the best: the right logos, the brand-name goods, more gigabytes. We seem to have lost a sense of what is sufficient. Benedict tells us to be content with what we have. When books are given out in the classroom, do you want the newest or can you be content with the one that is falling to bits? After all, does it matter as long as both have all the information you need? If, as a teacher, you can choose between two classrooms, do you opt for the one with the fancier overhead projector? Does it matter, provided both do the job? In a nutshell, Benedict says, be content with less than the best.

Prayer

Father, help us to be satisfied with what we have
and with what we are given.
Help us to be aware of the needs of others
and not to be always wanting what seems the best.
Help us to be generous in our giving and receiving.
Amen.

Chapter Section (Step 7)

It is good for me that you have humbled me, that I may learn your commandments [PSALM 119:71, 73]. (7:54)

Discussion

This is a difficult one, without a doubt. Not only are we to admit that we are unworthy but we are to believe it. This seems like grovelling! But it puts us in a position from where we can grow in humility. St. Benedict says that admitting that we are unworthy will free us from thinking of ourselves and others in a false light—of lying. It frees us to respect, revere and deal gently with others who have been unfortunate enough to have their own smallness come to light. In other words, do not give others a hard time even when it appears they deserve it. When we have an opportunity to be kind, let's use it.

Prayer

Lord, why do we sometimes give people a hard time?
Do we see our own faults in them?
Jesus, we need your gentleness
in dealing with each other and ourselves.
Amen.

Chapter Section (Step 8)

The eighth step of humility is to do nothing except what is encouraged by the common rule of the community or the example of the superiors. (7:55)

Discussion

Keep the rules of the school. They have been made by those wiser and we need to follow them or end up in chaos. If we think we know better and start to change things, we lose the opportunity to learn from others. It takes a great deal of time to learn all the secrets of life by ourselves. Students are to seek the example of teachers, teachers are to set the example, and actions speak louder than words. Our school, our living community has a great deal to teach us. Watch and listen. Accept that we need to learn from each other in the community.

Prayer

It is sometimes hard to do as we are told, God,
to keep the rules.
We pray that you will help us understand that
by following the example of those in authority
we will learn a great deal about ourselves and life.
We pray for those who teach, that they may be given
wisdom and guidance in their responsibilities.
Amen.

Food for Thought

It's not reading or learning the Rule that changes communities, but *living* it.

The Ladder Image

Chapter seven is difficult to carry out. At the beginning Benedict has given us the image of a ladder to help us through the Twelve Steps of Humility. In this segment I have added an exercise which will help students understand the image.

Chapter Section

...all exaltation is a kind of pride, against which the prophet indicates that he guards himself, saying: Lord my heart is not exalted nor are my eyes lifted up; nor have I walked in great things, nor in wonders above me [PSALM 131:1]. (7:2-3)

Discussion

This means...Know your place, don't get too big for your boots! It turns our values upside down. But if we want to please God then our values may need to change that much. We are raised up by going *down* the spiritual ladder. Yes, up is down and down is up. Read the story of Jacob's Ladder [GENESIS 28:12], in which angels go up and down the dream ladder between Earth and Heaven. The angels descend from God to raise us up.

Prayer

God our Father,
there are many things that we find difficult
to understand and to accept.
Help us to look again at what would please you,
and when it seems hard,
give us the strength to accept.
Amen.

Challenge

Draw a picture of a ladder, write UP at the bottom and
DOWN at the top. On one side list all the things that
make us go down from Heaven, and on the other write
a list of the things that raise us up. For example,
bullying, gossip, greed, arrogance, seeking praise, are
all things that keep us from God. In the way of the
world, these would be seen as steps up the ladder.
Whereas humility, unselfishly helping others, sharing
someone else's troubles, are all acts that take us closer
to God, but do not immediately appear to help us get on
in the world.

A symbol which helps us remember this principle is
that of the angels who are instructed to bring you from
the bottom of the ladder to Heaven. If you are already
at the top, they pass you by because you are in the
wrong place for the pick up!

Chapter Section

And the ladder thus erected is our life in the world, which, if the heart is humbled, is lifted up by the Lord to heaven. (7:8)

Discussion

A humble person is not a groveller, like the character Uriah Heap, created by Charles Dickens, but rather a person who doesn't ask for praise. When you are praised, accept the good words, but don't seek them. If you walk into a situation where you are unfairly treated, to answer back, to offer excuses, will often make things worse. To accept the situation and to be polite under pressure will in fact make your accuser think twice about their harsh words and actions. All this is very hard, but it does work. The Rule of Benedict has never failed a generation.

Prayer

Jesus, without being judgmental,
we pray for those who find it funny to belittle others
by using hurtful words and actions.
Give them and us the help we need to become
the people you want us to be.
Amen.

Chapter Section

Eternal life has been prepared for those who revere God. (7:11)

Discussion

I guess that only those who believe in God are interested in what is waiting for them! If we do love God, why don't we spend more of this life with Him, before we wonder about the next? When did we last spend some special, 'quality' time alone with God? God wants us to spend time with Him. Why shouldn't we want to spend time with our Friend?

Prayer

God, you are Almighty,
Jesus is our Brother
and the Holy Spirit is the one who gives us strength.
Help us to give you some time,
because you give us plenty.
Amen.

Chapter Section (Step 9)

A monk prohibits his tongue from speaking having restraint of speech unless asked a question [PSALM 34:14]. (7:56)

Discussion

When we are big-headed, it is usually shown in what we say, our ideas become the goal, our word is the last word. We are first into a conversation. Again, Benedict says that the way to humility is to listen, to learn and to be open to others. Humility is what enables the learned to learn from the wise. If we were to do this in class today, what a lot we would learn, and what a good day the teachers would have!

Prayer

Heavenly Father,
sometimes we think we will be heard
if we just keep talking.
Help us to value the art of listening,
and especially of listening to you.
Amen.

Challenge

In twos, sit facing each other and both talk at the same time. After a minute stop and see how much you have heard and understood of the other.

Chapter Section (Step 10)

Be not easily or promptly moved to laughter. For it is written: The fool raises his voice in laughter [SIRACH 21:23]. (7:59)

Discussion

So, Benedict was a bore and a misery! I think not. What he is saying is that we should laugh *with* a person, not *at* a person. Sexist jokes are not funny, disabilities, pornography, snide remarks and sarcasm are not funny. These say more about the tellers than the objects of their supposed fun. Sister Joan Chittister has something beautiful to say on the subject: "The humble person never uses speech to grind another person to dust. The humble person cultivates a soul in which everyone is safe. A humble person handles the presence of the other with soft hands, velvet heart, and an unveiled mind." In a nutshell, never ridicule.

Prayer

Lord, we thank you for the gift of laughter.
May we use it only to cheer people up
and to bring joy.
May we resist the temptation to laugh at
the shortcomings and misfortunes of others.
Give us the humility to see that others
make up what is lacking in me.
Amen.

Chapter Section (Step 11)

As it is written: The wise are known by their few words. (7:61)

Discussion

Benedict suggests we tread gently among the lives around us. When we know our own places, we can value others. If we allow God to be God, we can stop acting as if we were God ourselves. In a nutshell: speak kindly, speak gently.

Prayer

Father, you are our God and we are your children.
Help us to treat all around us with respect,
for we are brothers and sisters
and equal in your sight.
Amen.

Chapter Section (Step 12)

The monk, not only in his heart, but by means of his own body always indicates his humility to those who see him...whether sitting, walking or standing...(7:6-63)

Discussion

This whole chapter, although demanding, does not say that we have to be perfect. But it does tell us to be honest about what we are, for then we will come to know God. If we can respect others, if we can let God work in us so we can become the people He wants us to be, then we will have rediscovered humility for ourselves and our community will benefit. Humility is a lost virtue which the world is calling out for. Follow this difficult chapter and you will be doing your bit!

Prayer

Father, you have given us your Holy Spirit
so that we can have the wisdom to grow in love.
Help us to call upon that Spirit
so that we can become
the people you want us to be.
Amen.

Food for Thought

Humility has the same root as the word 'humus.' Humus is old organic material that has decomposed and has become a rich substance that enables good growth in a garden. When humus is used to replace poor soil and weeds, growth can be spectacular!

CHAPTERS 8—18: DETAILS OF SERVICES AND THEIR CONTENT

Introduction

These chapters give great detail about the community prayer life of a monastery, precisely which Psalms are to be sung and when, and so on. Though the examination of these chapters is brief here, schools which hold regular community prayer services will find St. Benedict's suggestions helpful from time to time.

Chapter Section

As the Prophet says: Seven times a day have I spoken your praise [PSALM 119:164]. (16:1)

Discussion

Today the school bell or buzzer gives us some idea of the discipline and time spent in prayer and praise during the time of St. Benedict. Even today some monasteries and convents pray together much as Benedict prescribed. Imagine if each time the school bell rang it meant we were to go to the chapel to pray. How long would we last? This routine, although it may have been adapted to a greater or lesser degree, is still at the heart of Benedictine life. Throughout the world, the daily 'Offices' structure the lives of those called to serve God in the footsteps of St. Benedict.

Although we may not be called to the monastic life, we are reminded that a quick morning or evening prayer, or a prayer at roll-call is not going to produce spiritual giants, any more than a quick 'hello' or 'good-bye' is going to produce a deep friendship with a fellow human being. These detailed chapters on prayer, praise and worship and its organization show us the importance of time spent with God our Creator.

Could we consider praying seven times a day? If prayer were to be offered at the beginning and at the end of each school lesson, grace said before the midday meal and then a short prayer offered before the homeward journey, we may have gone a long way to fulfilling the prayer of the Psalmist. Would our days be better or worse for having given those extra moments to God?

The prayer attributed to St. Benedict is exactly what is needed at the beginning of everything we do. This short formula may make all the difference to the success of a lesson. It can't do any harm and it may do a lot of good.

Prayer

We pray, Lord, that everything we do
may be prompted by your inspiration
so that every prayer and work of ours
may begin from you
and be brought by you to completion.
Amen.

(Silence for personal prayer)

—Let us praise God
—And give thanks.

CHAPTER 19:
THE DISCIPLINE OF CHANTING THE PSALMS

Introduction

After several chapters about the Divine Office (services), the times and the order of saying and chanting the Psalms, Benedict sums up everything in this chapter.

Chapter Section

...and thus stand to chant psalms in such a way that our mind and voice are in concord with each other. (19:7)

Discussion

The Psalms are perhaps the most underrated part of scripture in our schools. At Mass they are 'the thing that has the response.' But they are the most sublime hymns of praise. They speak wonderfully to the individual as they are recited in community. The monks of Benedict's day recited all hundred and fifty daily. They were memorized and chanted during work as well as in choir. Today, not all the Psalms are said. The violent ones are omitted, and as many as one hundred and thirty are chanted in a four or five week cycle. In the Psalms we feel that God is speaking to his people. In times of joy or sorrow, the Psalms have just the right words.

Prayers Before a Lesson

Lord, I offer all my work and actions of this lesson to you.
Guide me, direct me, control me and help me
so that at the end of the lesson I can be pleased
that I have pleased you.
Amen.

•

Lord, during the day help us to turn to you with our
problems and difficulties.
We try to dedicate our lives to you, but it is difficult.
So, we ask for your help and forgiveness.
Amen.

Chapter Section

We believe that the Divine Presence is everywhere, and the eyes of the Lord in every place look upon the good and the evil. [PROVERBS 15:3] We especially believe this without any doubt when we are assisting at the Work of God. (19:1, 2)

Discussion

The Work of God is the Divine Office, prayer. How often do our minds wander during prayer? We bow our heads, close our eyes and clasp our hands. All these actions are to help us concentrate. When we hear the words, 'Let us pray,' do we try to concentrate in order to communicate with God? We do not like being distracted when we are on the phone to our friends; are we as keen to concentrate when we are communicating with God? Are we as eager to listen to God as we are to our friends? When we do give time to prayer, we can use our own words or use familiar prayers—which can be handy when we can't think of what to say!

Prayer

> Lord, we are always in your presence.
> Help us to give you our full attention.
> Amen.

Challenge

Read or pray Psalm 139. Find different translations and see which one 'speaks' best to you. The *New Jerusalem Bible* has a heading describing each Psalm so that an appropriate one can be found for a particular occasion. Remember, Benedictine spirituality is not concerned with who can pray for the longest time, who can recite the most, but it does emphasize that every part of our lives can be a prayer and that in the Psalms we can find God.

Chapter Section

Therefore let us consider how we ought to behave before the Holy One and His angels, and thus stand to chant psalms in such a way that our mind and voice are in concord with each other. (19: 6,7)

Discussion

Let us consider again, how do we behave at prayer time, at Mass, in chapel? These situations need serious thought. Not only can we be distracted but we can distract others too. Can we do anything to improve our behavior so that we and others can become more aware of the presence of God? Do we think about what we are saying? Is our 'Amen' really a response of agreement with what has been said? Are we just paying lip-service, or are we part of the communication between God and ourselves?

We do well to remind ourselves that prayer is a developing relationship, not a formula of 'vain repetition.'

Prayer

God our Creator, we are always in your presence.
We ask for the grace to give our full attention to you,
especially when we come to worship you.
Help us to listen to you and not only to ask for things.
Amen.

CHAPTER 20: REVERENCE IN PRAYER

Introduction

To round off all he has to say about prayer, St. Benedict has something he especially wants to be made clear.

Chapter Section

And we know that it is not on account of our wordiness that we are heard, but rather through purity of heart and tears of compunction. And therefore prayer ought to be brief and pure, unless it happens to be prolonged by a sentiment inspired by divine grace. (20:3,4)

Discussion

Again, as in Chapter 7 (on Humility), Benedict suggest our prayers should be to the point. We are not heard for our many words. After all, God does know what our needs are even before we ask! There is no need for lengthy explanations, God understands perfectly. Benedict does not give us a method or formula for prayer. He gives us guidelines and the rest is between God and ourselves. We do not need lots of time for prayer, but we do need some. And the time we give to God should be quality time, we should concentrate so that 'our minds are in harmony with our bodies.'

Prayer

God our Creator, you give so much to each one of us
that there is nothing we can offer to you,
except perhaps some time.
Help us to give you quality time and concentration.
Amen.

CHAPTER 21: THE DEANS OF THE COMMUNITY

Introduction

Perhaps this is not a chapter for the whole school, but certainly it is for the senior managers. For those who have the wisdom and humility to seek advice of the Master of Community, details can be found in any translation of his Rule.

Chapter Section

If the community is large, there should be chosen from it those of good reputation and a holy way of life to be appointed deans. They are to carefully oversee their deaneries [groups of ten]... The ones chosen should be those with whom the abbot may confidently share his burdens. (21:1-3)

Discussion

The one in charge of a school has innumerable responsibilities. This chapter shows the practical organization Benedict advocates. It presupposes that the one in charge has the wisdom and confidence to share responsibilities. It also removes the temptation to absolute power. Benedictine spirituality uses authority to weld a community, not to fracture it.

Prayers

God our Creator, help us to realize that
you are in ultimate control of this community.
Give to us, your servants,
wisdom to guide your community according to your will.
Amen.

•

We give you thanks, Almighty God, for our community.
May we who have auhority use our talents to your glory
And, forgetting self and power,
dedicate our lives to your service.
Amen.

CHAPTER 23: PUNISHMENT

Introduction

(Chapter 22 deals with sleeping arrangements). Regarded as having written the most gentle of monastic rules, St. Benedict still devotes quite a large proportion of it to punishment. His methods may not be acceptable today, but his ideas on what is punishable are sound. In the end, those who will not accept correction and who continually damage the community, must leave.

Chapter Section

If any brother is found to be contumacious, or disobedient or proud, or a grumbler or in any way has contempt for the Holy Rule and the precepts of his seniors, let him, according to Our Lord's precept, be admonished...(23:1, 2)

Discussion

If any member of a school community is found to be breaking a rule of that community, then the consequences must be faced. Breaking a rule, be it talking in class, or a more serious fault such as stealing, rudeness, fighting, has its punishment. Admitting the fault and correcting it are part of a process that helps us heal and grow. Denial—"It wasn't me, I didn't do it!"—offers no solution or growth. But saying, "I did it. I know it was wrong, I'm sorry and I'll try to be better," indicates the attitude that will help healing and progress. None of this is meant to be easy, but it is right!

Prayer

Jesus, we know that there are times
when we stray from the right path.
Help us to face the consequences of our actions.
Help us to see healing and growth
as we face up to correction.
Amen.

Chapter Section

...let the wrongdoer according to Our Lord's precept, be admonished once or twice in private by his seniors [MATTHEW 18:15, 16]. (23:2)

Discussion

St. Benedict gives chances before punishment becomes severe. You get the chance to improve, not an opportunity to get away with doing wrong again! Here is the chance to put things right. We already know what is right and acceptable and we should behave accordingly, if we do not then we obviously need help. So, we are warned privately. Benedict is sensitive towards people and gives us a second or even third chance. But there are limits to what a community will stand for. When the limits are exceeded, punishment has to take place.

Prayer

Lord God, if we do wrong, help us to see
the structures that are in place
to help us correct our behavior.
May we take opportunities for correction
as gifts that will help us to grow
to become the people you want us to be.
Amen.

Chapter Section

If he does not amend he should be publicly rebuked in the presence of all. (23:3)

Discussion

The quiet word in the ear, "Don't do that..." but the hint is not taken and the reprimand has to become stronger, "Stand up..." Under such circumstances it is good that we are told off in front of the class, year group or even the whole school! What Benedict wants us to see is that if it is the community rule which we have broken, then the community should witness the punishment. We should always remember that the matter is in our own hands: if we take the hint from the start and do not break the rules, then we avoid getting punished.

Prayer

Lord Jesus, sometimes we are so weak
that we just go over the top.
We do not stop to think what effect our wrong deeds
can have on the whole community.
Help us to turn to you
for help and direction in all we do.
Amen.

Chapter Section

If he still refuses to be corrected, provided he understands what this penalty signifies, he should be subjected to excommunication. (23:4)

Discussion

Yes, Benedict even threw monks out of their monastery! The community must be protected. If, when we have had all the warnings, detentions, etcetera, but still continue with the wrongdoings, we may be on the way to the big penalty. In school terms, this is exclusion. It will be made very clear why you have ended up outside! To understand our faults and wrongdoings is essential if we are going to change. We need to know what has to be changed. When we do change, we can then be accepted, forgiven and welcomed back into the community.

Prayer

Lord, may we come to realize that by doing wrong,
we are damaging not only ourselves
but also our community.
Help us to change when we receive warnings,
so that we will not be excluded from our community.
Amen.

CHAPTERS 25–27: SERIOUS FAULTS

Introduction

These chapters are a means to healing and growth rather than something harsh and sadistic. Punishment is always meant to heal, not destroy, and these chapters are for those whose responsibility is to administer it. Remember that unruly, ill-disciplined people as well as holy hard-workers sought Benedict's community—a similar mix to that found in the classroom! The methods and suggestions offered here might be different from anything you have considered before. Please read them with an open mind and a will to try a well-tested method from the sixth century.

Chapter Section

That brother who is guilty of a more serious fault is to be suspended both from the common table and the oratory. (25:1)

Discussion

How serious is serious? A serious fault damages the community and the individual and puts the wrongdoer beyond the community rule. The wholesome reason for isolating a pupil is to give him space to think about the wrong and about how to return to the community. This can be far more effective than shouting, breeding resentment, providing justification for further confrontation—all things which can develop from harsh, thoughtless punishment.

Prayer

Father, to be sent out, to be removed from our friends
is often a humiliating and lonely experience.
We pray that in being alone we may find a solution
to our anti-social actions.
May we use any space and time given to us
to help us grow and to become better.
Amen.

Chapter Section

If a brother presumes without permission from the abbot to associate in any way with an excommunicated brother, or to speak with him, or to send him a message, he will incur the same kind of punishment of excommunication. (26:1,2)

Discussion

What was it we said about this *gentle* Rule of Benedict? At first, this seems very spiteful—but wait! The previous section pointed out the importance of exclusion, in giving the wrongdoer time to think, to heal. If it is interrupted by someone interfering, so that the healing and reflection become more difficult, then the person who interferes also needs time to think about their actions in isolation.

Prayer

Lord Jesus, help us not to interfere
in the healing work of punishment,
but to help those who are trying to come to terms
with their behavior,
by allowing them space and time to reflect.
Amen.

Chapter Section

It is with all solicitude that the abbot should care for delinquent brothers, for it is not the healthy who have need of a physician, but those who are sick. [MATTHEW 9:12]. (27:1)

Discussion

The abbot is, in our case, is the one who has issued the punishment. To send someone away, to isolate him simply to get rid of a problem would not be showing the utmost concern. Benedict says that the intention should never be to crush the person being corrected, but to show concern for their growth, to enable them to reclaim their place in the community. The purpose of punishment is to enable the person punished to get life into perspective and to start afresh. Benedict says quite clearly that those issuing punishment are to be seen as doctors and shepherds tending the weak and carrying the lost, they are not to be drill-sergeants or impresarios.

Prayer

Lord, with authority comes the duty to punish.
We ask for wisdom when we have to punish.
May we be always guided by a desire to help,
to cure, to develop and heal.
We ask that our actions produce people
who are part of a Christ-centered community.
Amen.

CHAPTERS 28–30: MORE ABOUT CORRECTION

Introduction

Benedict devotes plenty of time to punishment, which shows how keen he was on correction and healing. The right kind of correction, always with a view to growth, is extremely important in community life.

Chapter Section

If he then does not correct himself, or even, inflamed with pride, he wishes to defend his actions, then the abbot should act as a wise physician...(28:2)

Discussion

Benedict realized that there are those in the community whose pride makes them defend a wrong action by saying things like: "It wasn't me!" And, "I know what I did was wrong, but I don't care!" This sort of attitude does no-one any good, it damages the person in the wrong, and it damages the community to which each of us has responsibility. Benedict says that serious faults, which cause serious damage, require serious punishment. If good cannot come out of bad, then the whole community can become infected.

Prayer

For those who cannot face up to their wrong,
we pray, God, that they will turn to you,
and find forgiveness, support and understanding
in the community.
Amen.

Chapter Section

If a brother who from his own evil action departs from the monastery, then wishes to return, he should first promise the complete amendment of that which caused his departure. (29:1)

Discussion

Here, Benedict recognizes the indecision and uncertainty involved in leaving and returning to the community, and tries to contain it positively so that in the end the right way may be discerned. We must learn that there is a price to pay for coming and going. We must start anew with a clean sheet. Everyone else in the community will have moved on, and we must make every effort to catch up. The people of the community must welcome the person returning and know that it is unhelpful to over-react to the slightest fault. Comments such as "You'll never change, you'll never learn!" are to be avoided. Remember Jesus tells us to forgive another 'seventy times seven.'

Prayer

Lord, when we are given a fresh start,
help us to concentrate on making
the best of the opportunity.
Amen.

Chapter Section

Every age and intellectual capacity should receive the measure proper to it. Thus, with regard to young adolescents, or those who lack the ability to understand the significance of the penalty of excommunication... (30:1-2)

Discussion

Often, children do not realize the seriousness of being excluded. It needs to be made very clear, otherwise the effect of the punishment will be lost and healing will not take place.

It would be worthwhile for every teacher to read the chapters on punishment in the Rule in their entirety. The methods and ideas, while no longer novel, could be the basis of significant change in the way punishment is regarded. For instance,there is the idea that punishment and humility are linked, and if punishment is carried out humbly and accepted humbly, then it does produce growth.

Prayer

Jesus, help us to see the point of punishment.
May we take responsibility for our wrongdoing
and learn to grow from its consequences.
Amen.

Food for Thought

This incident occurred in the school where I was chaplain. The Angelus bell outside the Chapel is usually respected, but if it is rung as a prank then the offender has to clean it. I spotted one lad running away after ringing the bell, told him he had to clean it and he entered on the task with enthusiasm. When he had finished, I complimented him on a job well done and he thanked me. I asked him if he realized that he had thanked me for a punishment. He smiled and said, "Oh yes!" He knew he had done wrong, but was pleased to have made proper amends.
—Thank you, Benedict, from both of us!

CHAPTER 31: THE CELLARER

Introduction

Cellarer comes from a Latin word for 'storeroom.' So the Cellarer is the person who looks after all the equipment and distributes stores in the monastery.

Chapter Section

As monastery cellarer there should be chosen from the community one who is wise, of mature character, temperate, not an excessive eater, not haughty, not turbulent, not harmful, not sluggish, not wasteful...
(31:1)

Discussion

Having concentrated on how we should behave towards people, Benedict now turns to how we chould deal with material things. This will be a chapter of great value in school. Sometimes the things around us, provided for our use, but not bought by us, are treated with little respect. This is not only wasteful, costly and selfish, but often reflects the way we treat people. In working with this chapter there is opportunity to draw attention to the care of things that are provided for us, to understand their cost, and the need to preserve them for others.

Prayer

Father, we thank you for all that we have been given.
Help us to treat gifts with respect,
as if they are gifts from you.
Amen.

Chapter Section

He is to do nothing without an order from the abbot. He is to keep custody over his orders... (31:4,5)

Discussion

Once again, Benedict is pointing out that with every position there is responsibility, and we must be careful not to forget that we are all answerable to a higher authority. We must guard against misuse of power. The key lies in being moderate and fair in our dealings with others. For instance, if we are given things to share with others, do we save the best for ourselves? Do we give a larger portion to our friends? Have you experienced such situations in the classroom, at lunch time, or on the playing fields?

Prayer

Lord, help us to be fair in all our dealings.
Help us to act with responsibility in every situation.
Amen.

Challenge

In small groups, share some experiences and answer these questions: Have you done any of these unfair things? Have you seen others doing them? Is it easier to see unfairness in others than in ourselves? Remember the work you have done on Humility!

Chapter Section

If the community is large, helpers are to be given to the cellarer, thanks to whose assistance he may retain a peaceful soul while fulfilling the office committed to him... So that no-one is perturbed or saddened in the house of God. (31:17, 19)

Discussion

Accepting help is sometimes humbling, we all like to think that we can cope with everything that comes our way. But if we accept help as necessary we can complete a task without stress or anxiety, and everyone benefits. Remember that St. Benedict's monks were a motley crowd of very different people, and it was his Rule which molded them into a thriving spiritual community. A peaceful approach to our tasks is an important factor in building community.

Prayer

Father, help us to accept the assistance offered,
especially when it teaches us humility.
We like to feel that we can go it alone.
But keep us aware of the need we have of you
and of one another.
Amen.

Chapter Section

Above all else the Cellarer is to have humility: when he has nothing material to give to one who makes a request, he is to offer at least a kind word. As it is written, A kind word is higher than the best gift [SIRACH 18:17]. (31:13-14)

Discussion

We are back to the subject of humility, and this chapter is as much about relationships, the heart of the community, as it is about things. Think about the use and abuse of power, which can be a destructive force in any community: am I tempted to make people look small, do I try to dominate them? Do I try to make people dependent on me? Do I irritate them? Benedict says again how important peace is to the human heart. So, the Cellarer, under the pressure of a demanding job is told to give himself peace and the time to consider his own needs. Make time for peace, make time for prayer. —"No peace, no God. Know peace, know God."

Prayer

Father, help us always to treat each other
with respect and kindness.
We pray for peace in our hearts and minds.
Release us from the stress that destroys our peace.
We ask for the gift of peace that only you can give.
Amen.

Food for Thought

This chapter contains a much-quoted injunction that all equipment should be treated with the same care as the sacred vessels used in Mass. If we did this, think how long things would last! Think of the way we treat chairs, desks, books, and look at the mess we create every day—the litter, the chewing gum. Do we have any regard for those who clean up after us?

CHAPTER 32: TOOLS AND GOODS

Chapter Section

Of these items the abbot is to keep a list, so that as the brothers are successively assigned to different tasks, he will know what he gives out and what he receives back. (32:3)

Discussion

Everything we have is on loan and eventually has to be handed back. When you borrow something do you return it in the same (or better) condition as you received it—or do you perhaps even forget to hand it back? Think of all that we have received from God. One day we will have to account for how we have used or abused, hidden or developed our talents, our gifts.

Our prayer is part of an offertory hymn. Can you remember any more of it?

Prayer

> All that I am,
> all that I do,
> all that I ever have
> I offer now to you.
> Amen.

Chapter Section

Anyone who treats the goods of the monastery improperly or negligently is to be corrected. (32:4)

Discussion

This chapter is a warning, just in case anyone should think that following the spiritual life is an excuse to ignore the things of the world. Again, Benedict tells us that the ordinary things we use are to be treated carefully, with respect.

Prayer

Father, we have so much.
Sometimes we forget to appreciate
the things we have been given.
We pray that from our position of plenty
we be generous in our giving
to those who have little.
Amen.

Challenge

Make a list of the things in your possession: your bike, your computer, your clothes, your shoes, and so on. Against each item give yourself a grade or mark—A, B, C, D or F, according to how you take care of it.

Now think about how much waste there is in our world, think about our throwaway society. And think about how you can be more economical with the things you use. Look around you as you go about the school and see what has been wasted or spoiled. How can you make a special effort not to contribute to the waste?

Chapter Section

If he does not amend, he is to be subjected to the discipline of the Rule. (32:5)

Discussion

St. Benedict does not fool around, evil practices should be punished! He is urging us to be careful. It is not so much the possessions themselves that are of concern, but that they can become an obstacle in the good relationship between ourselves and others. The things that we possess can lead to greed and competitiveness. Benedict advises us that such an attitude be cut out before it has a chance to grow.

Prayer

Jesus, by your example,
help us not to place too much importance
in what we have.
Help us to see the importance in who we are
and in how much you love us.
Amen.

Food for Thought

• Do you think of others before yourself?

• How important is it that you follow the latest fashion or fad?

• Your belongings are not what make you. What do you think does make you?

• Think of something that you have always wanted. How did you feel when you got it? How long did that feeling last?

• Think of something you really want. Why do you want it?

• God is always ready to give himself to us in Mass and Holy Communion. How ready are you to give yourself to God?

CHAPTER 33: PRIVATE OWNERSHIP

Introduction

St. Benedict says that the more we own, the more we are tied down. Giving up things does not deprive us, it frees us.

Chapter Section

...No one may presume to give or receive anything without the abbot's order, nor to have anything as their own...(33:2-3)

Discussion

This is a very difficult chapter to understand, especially in these days when apparently the more you own, the better off you are. How often when we own something do we find ourselves tied to it? For instance, if you own a pet and want to go away for a few days, you have to to make arrangements to take it with you or for it to be looked after. You are tied by ownership.

Prayer

Father, in this world it seems that
possessions make us better.
But we know that Jesus and St. Benedict
had very little to call their own,
so they were free to dedicate their lives to you.
Help us to understand that having very little
can free us to serve you.
Amen.

Chapter Section

All things are to be held in common by all, as it is written, so that no one may say or presume that anything is his own [ACTS 4:32]. But if anyone is found engaging in this most destructive vice, he is to be admonished once or twice: if he does not amend, he is to be subjected to correction. (33:6-8)

Discussion

Joan Chittister OSB, has an interesting thought in this regard: "Common ownership and personal dependence are the foundation of mutual respect." Knowing that we are dependent on each other, we should rely on each other. To be able to say, "I need you and you need me," is much healthier than saying, "I don't need anyone, I can go it alone." In community life we genuinely need one another. Let's not pretend that we don't!

Prayer

Lord Jesus, help each one of us to see
the need we have for the other.
Help us to realize that you are in each one of us
and that we should look for you in everyone we meet.
Amen.

CHAPTER 34: WHETHER ALL SHOULD RECEIVE NECESSARY THINGS EQUALLY

Introduction

We have had a taste now of more than half of St. Benedict's Rule. The preceding chapters looked at the individual and the community and showed how they are interdependent and share friendship with God. The following chapters show in practical terms what love asks and what love gives.

At a study weekend with Esther de Waal, the writer on Benedictine spirituality, we agreed that the Rule should carry a health warning: The Rule changes people if we let it, it challenges them and, if it is working, probably hurts! As has been said of the Gospel: 'It comforts the afflicted and afflicts the comfortable.'

Chapter Section

As it is written, Distribution was made to each according to his need [ACTS 4:35]. (34:1)

Discussion

Benedict quotes the Acts of the Apostles and makes clear that though our needs will be met, what we want is not necessarily what we get! We should be content with what we are given rather than desire what we do not have. And we should be pleased with what others in the community receive, no envy or greed, not wanting the best for ourselves at the expense of others.

Prayer

Father, you know what we need before we even ask.
Help us to trust you and each other
and to be thankful for all your gifts to us.
Amen.

Chapter Section

Above all, the evil of grumbling must not appear for any reason, through any word or sign whatever. (34:6)

Discussion

This asks that we have true concern for each other. No one should envy another. Grumbling is the enemy! It was the Pharisees, the strong, who, jealous of the mercy shown to the weak, criticized Jesus' love. What Benedict intends is that our love be unconditional, open, truthful, trusting, non-judgmental. How can we live in community successfully if we do not think of each other before ourselves?

Prayers

In silence, let us pray for each other.

•

Jesus, you showed us the way of unconditional love.
We pray for the strength to trust
that in following your way
your community will benefit.
Amen.

CHAPTER 35: THE KITCHEN SERVERS

Chapter Section

The brothers are to serve one another; thus no one is to be excused from kitchen duties...For the feeble, however, assistance is to be procured so they do not become discouraged. (35:1,3)

Discussion

The kitchen is central to any community. It is probably one of our favorite places, a place from where we are served. We are probably very keen on eating but not too excited about serving and washing up. But as in Benedict's community, we should all serve each other, and not just in the kitchen. We are to regard it as a privilege to serve: no moaning if we are asked to give out the books, to put away the chairs. If we are not prepared to serve each other cheerfully then we can hardly claim to be a team, a family, a community.

Prayer

Jesus, you were prepared to kneel at the feet
of your friends and wash their feet.
Teach us what service is.
Help us to be willing to serve as well as to be served.
We pray for our kitchen staff who serve us daily.
Amen.

Chapter Section

They are to wash the towels with which the brothers wipe their hands and feet. (35:8)

Discussion

Yuk! What kind of disgusting job is this? Italy can have a hot climate, and here we are, washing out a week's worth of sweaty towels. Benedict expects no less of everyone in his community. Loving service is not always a delight! But it is not the dirty towels that are our focus, it is the service to each other that is important. Love gives you the chance to perform tasks that you would not normally do. Everyone takes their turn, even the person in charge must not miss the opportunity to serve.

Prayer

Jesus, help us to realize that serving each other,
while it may not seem an honor or privilege,
gives us the opportunity to show our love.
Amen.

Chapter Section

An hour before the meal the weekly servers are to receive, over and above the usual allowance, a drink and a piece of bread... (35:12)

Discussion

Here we see Benedict the practical, Benedict the understanding. How would you like to serve food to others when you are hungry? You would probably resent it. But to serve is not an endurance test, simply allow that the edge be taken off the hunger of the servers and the problem is solved. St. Benedict had an understanding of human psychology before it was invented!

Prayer

Lord, help us to understand
that the people who are in charge
have our best interests at heart.
Make all leaders worthy of their position
and give them a sense of loving responsibility.
Amen.

Chapter Section

The server ending his week is to say this verse: Blessed are you, Lord God, who have helped me and consoled me [DANIEL 3:52; PSALM 86:17]; and having said this three times, the one ending his service is to receive the blessing. The one beginning his service then continues, saying: O God come to my assistance, O Lord make haste to help me [PSALM 70:2]. (35:16, 17)

Discussion

Those who have been serving and those who are about to serve say a verse of scripture in thanks. Those who are beginning know they need help. The prayer of St. Benedict reads, 'We pray, Lord, that everything we do may be prompted by your inspiration...' Do we acknowledge that we need God's help in everything we do? If God has created the universe, then helping us will be no problem for him!

Prayer

Lord, we pray that we remember
to begin every task by asking for your help,
and to end every task by offering thanks.
Help us to know that you are interested
in everything we attempt,
and to know that with you, the job will be better.
Amen.

Challenges

•If you are planning to do something today that is worrying you, ask God for help.

•Think of something that you enjoy doing—a sport, playing music, reading. God is interested in all that you do. Ask for God's blessing on your activity.

• Think of the people who serve you every day, people who make your life easier: postmen, shopkeepers, bus-drivers, kitchen staff. Thank them when you see them and give them a smile.

CHAPTER 36: THE SICK

Chapter Section

Care of the sick must rank before and above everything, so that truly they may be served as Christ himself, for he said, I was sick and you visited me... [MATTHEW 25:36]. (36:1, 2)

Discussion

We all have days when we do not feel well. Thankfully, these days pass for most of us. In this chapter of the Rule we are told to treat people who are sick with special care, for we are treating Christ when we minister to them. Let us then have all the more consideration for people who have illnesses or disabilities that do not go away. No one should ever be ridiculed or ignored because they are ill or weak. Remember that we all have weaknesses, and some of us have disabilities which are less visible than others.

Prayer

We pray especially for those in our community who are ill. We remember those being cared for at home or in hospital.
Bless and strengthen those who care for the sick.
(Pause to mention names of people who are ill).
We offer these prayers to you, God, healer of us all.
Amen.

Chapter Section

Yet the sick are to be patiently borne, because from such as these a more abundant reward is acquired. The abbot shall therefore exercise the greatest care that they do not suffer any neglect. (36:5,6)

Discussion

This section implies that caring for the sick is a God-given opportunity to serve. How often do we see this part of life? How do you react to illness, either your own or that of others? Unfortunately, the world seems to favor the strong and the powerful but Christ and St. Benedict give special attention to those who are weak, and tell us that we are to follow their example.

Prayer

Jesus, our example and guide, help us to see
an opportunity of giving love and service
to those who are in need.
We pray that we will always look with kindness
on those whom we are asked to care for.
Amen.

CHAPTER 37: THE AGED AND CHILDREN

Introduction

Probably the school staff think of the students as children and the students think of the staff as elderly! Whether or not this is precisely the case, St. Benedict is saying that these categories should not be overlooked in the special care that we ideally devote to each other in all phases of life.

Chapter Section

Their weakness should always be considered, and they are in no way required to adhere to the full rigor of the Rule... (37:2)

Discussion

Let us remember that, for example, at the beginning of the school year or semester, there are many young new members to welcome to the community. It is now their community and we who have been here before must make sure their introduction is a happy experience. This is not a time to throw our weight around just because we are older or bigger than the new students. Jesus said, 'For in as much as you do it unto the least of my friends, you do it to me' [MATTHEW 25:40]. Treat each other with the respect and care and tolerance with which you would wish to be treated, in this way we will be forming our Christian community.

Prayer

Jesus, you never made anyone feel unwelcome or small.
We pray that when we find people in our community
who are bewildered or afraid,
help us to give them a hand and a friendly smile.
Amen.

CHAPTER 38: THE READER FOR THE WEEK

Introduction

In many monasteries and convents a spiritual book is read aloud at meal times. In St. Benedict's day it was usually the Bible. Meals are a time for filling the soul as well as the stomach! Benedict says that the reader must be a good reader so that those listening are not distracted by mistakes—a good reason for being selective. Remember that we have different talents, if we were all brilliant readers but none of us could play football, life would be pretty dull!

Chapter Section

At the brother's table there always should be reading, but this should not be done carelessly by one who simply grabs for the book and reads, rather let the reader be one who begins a whole week's service on Sunday. (38:1)

Discussion

I doubt that anyone who read aloud in a noisy school dining-room would be heard—even with a PA system. The louder we are, the louder others shout to be heard above us. I am not suggesting eating meals in silence, but it would be good if we stopped talking long enough to listen to our friends, our teachers, our supervisors.

Prayer

God our Creator, you created the world from nothing.
There is no mention of you creating noise
—*we* seem to be pretty good at that.
We ask you to make us aware of the noise that we create
and we ask that you help us to bring peace,
to a corner of your world today.
Amen.

Chapter Section

...and this verse is to be said three times in the oratory by all after the reader begins it: O Lord, open my lips, and my mouth shall declare your praise [PSALM 51:17]; and thus receiving the blessing he begins his service of reading. (38:3-4)

Discussion

If only we allowed God to open our mouths, how much better would be the things that came out! Can you imagine God helping us to curse or lie or to show disrespect, to say, "Shut up! Get lost!" —or to say anything remotely hurtful or rude? If we could hear ourselves speak sometimes, we would be ashamed. The pity is that sometimes we are not ashamed when we *do* hear ourselves. If someone tells us to stop using foul language, for instance, we are likely to continue with added vigor. How do we stop the downward spiral? Be aware that God can open our lips, as God does when we say kind, loving, generous, forgiving, friendly words. And, yes, funny words too. God likes to laugh.

Prayer

Holy Spirit, gentle teacher of wisdom,
help us to control our tongues today.
May we use them to be kind, helpful and supportive.
Help us to see that we can make a difference
to this community by thinking before we speak.
Help us also in our prayer
so that we can become the people you want us to be.
Amen.

Challenge

Read St. Paul's letter to James 3:5-11, in which there are several metaphors describing the way we talk and how we may control it.

Chapter Section

And total silence is to be kept, so that no whispering or voice may be heard there except that of the reader alone. (38:5)

Discussion

I doubt that there is any teacher who needs to be especially recommended to this passage! One suggestion: silence is not simply an absence of noise, so it might be constructive to say to the students, "Let's have some silence so that we can think about..." In the monastery silence is preserved for listening to God. As teachers in a church school we have a duty to lead each other to God. Silence is golden, and silence filled with God is infinitely more precious. Joan Chittister says, "The spiritual nourishment of an entire people is in our hands."

Prayer

God our Father, help us to see that silence
is not simply an absence of noise,
but an opportunity to listen
to you, our teachers, our friends, our parents, ourselves.
Give us silence in our busy day
and help us to fill that silence usefully.
Amen.

Challenge

Go somewhere on your own, perhaps the chapel, and be still and silent—not because you are lonely, but because you have chosen to be by yourself. Then, just listen. Listen to what? Just listen. Do not pray or fill your head with words, just listen. Listen for as long as you can.

CHAPTER 39: THE MEASURE OF FOOD

Chapter Section

We believe it will suffice for the daily meal...that there be on all tables two dishes of cooked food on account of the variety of infirmities: so that he who is not able to eat one may make his meal of the other... And if there are any fruit or young vegetables, a third dish is to be added. A liberal pound of bread should suffice each day... (39:1-4)

Discussion

These monks did not go hungry! St. Benedict makes sure that food is plentiful, simple and pleasing. He expected the monks to work, study and pray hard. For that you need the energy obtained from food. Do we eat to get the energy we need for work, play, study and prayer? Or do we eat simply because it is time to eat? Do we stuff in as much as we can, or do we eat the correct amount? Are we constantly worried about getting fat? Benedict's Rule is one of balance. We eat the right thing at the right time for the right reason. And do we thank God for our food? The practice of saying grace before and after meals has practically disappeared since cafeteria catering became common. However, you can still say grace privately or with your friends at the dinner table. If you are thanking God, you are on the right track!

Prayer

Lord, we thank you for the food we are about to eat,
thank you for those who have prepared it.
Help us to think of those who will not eat today.
Amen.

Chapter Section

...provided that before all else overindulgence is avoided, and that no monk suffers indigestion. For nothing is more contrary to all things Christian than overindulgence. As Our Lord says, See that your hearts are not weighed down through overindulgence. [LUKE 21:34] (39:7-9)

Discussion

At one time or another, every one of us has eaten too much. Remember that extra-big burger you thought you could manage? That fancy restaurant meal that was just so good you just carried on eating? Benedict says that we should try to keep our minds in charge of our bodies. We know how lazy we feel when we have eaten too much, or how dangerous it is to exercise after a large meal. So we must take care of our bodies. In other words, don't be a pig!

Prayer

God, you have created enough food
for everyone in your world.
We seem to have got the distribution wrong.
Help us to be sensible about what we eat.
Help us to remember those in poor countries
and to give what we can when the opportunity arises.
Amen.

Challenge

Find where there is a collection box which you can put money in for CAFOD or OXFAM or another agency involved in relieving hunger. Think about donating more than what you have to spare. How about giving up something that you want so that someone can have what they need?

CHAPTER 40: THE PROPER AMOUNT OF DRINK

Introduction

St. Benedict suggests half a bottle of wine daily as being the proper amount—and who is going to disagree! There are questions, though, how big is the bottle? And can we save it up and have a party at the end of the week? But none of this is the point of the chapter, which is to stop grumbling and have self-control. It starts with a quote from the Bible.

Chapter Section

'Everyone has his proper gift from God: one this, another that' [I CORINTHIANS 7:7]: and it is therefore with some reluctance that we fix the measure for another. However... we believe that a hemina of wine for each will suffice each day. But those to whom God gives the strength to abstain should know that they will earn their proper reward. (40:1-4)

Discussion

If you were told that you could never have chocolate again, you would probably go to great lengths to sneak some. The idea behind this section is that, while you can have what you need, you may find that you do not need all or any of what you are given. St. Benedict's intention here is to stop grumbling. Think about going without something today. It does not have to be Lent for you to practice self-control. If it means you save money, give it to a good cause.

Prayer

God, our Creator, you give us so much
and in our society, usually we can get anything we want.
We pray for those people who have no water,
no food, no resources.
Help us, from our position of plenty,
to be aware of the needs of others.
Amen.

Chapter Section

But where local necessities are such that even the above-mentioned measure cannot be supplied, and in some cases there is much less or nothing at all, those who dwell there are to bless God and not murmur. (40:8)

Discussion

This is one of the most important pieces of advice that St. Benedict gives to his and every community. Grumbling, murmuring, is like acid, it corrodes. It can destroy a community very quickly. Read Psalm 106:24-27, in which the people who murmured against God are scattered in the wilderness. If we each of us fell down dead when we grumbled, there would not be many of us left. If you think about it, grumbling never does any good, so why do it? This chapter is a fine example of how, for the sake of the community, the Rule of St. Benedict has to be *lived,* not just read or pinned on a bulletin board.

Prayer

Here, God, take this thing that makes me grumble
and in return give me a heart that is open and positive.
Help me to think about the many things I have
that make me happy and satisfied.
Amen.

Challenge

Take a moment of silence and think about something that makes you grumble and feel dissatisfied. Then think about how much good the grumbling has done you. Now let it go. Hand it over to God.

Chapter Section

This we admonish above everything else: that they refrain from murmuring. (40:9)

Discussion

Complaints must be sorted out responsibly and quickly, or the grumbling will grow and corrode everything around it. For instance, if there is something you do not understand about your homework, make sure you find out a way to understand, as soon as you can. If it is not done now, the problem will be greater tomorrow. In the same way, if people feel aggrieved, they will try to get others to share their feelings and before you know it, everyone will be complaining. Sort it out. Now.

Prayer

Lord, we pray for everyone with problems
—and that means all of us.
We ask for the courage to deal with our problems
so that peace and harmony can be restored
to each of us and to the community.
Amen.

Food for Thought

Joan Chittister, in *Insights for the Ages* writes:

If Benedictine spirituality understands anything about life at all, it understands the corrosive effect of constant complaining. Complaining is the acid that shrivels our own souls and the soul of the community around us. Complaining is what shapes our mental set. Feelings, psychology tells us, do not affect thought. Thoughts affect feelings. What we allow ourselves to think is what we are really allowing ourselves to feel... What we see as negative, we make negative and feel negative about. What we are willing to think about in a positive way becomes positive. Complaining undermines the hope of a community and smothers possibility. Benedictine spirituality tells us to open our hearts and our minds to let grace come in from unlikely places.

CHAPTER 41: MEAL TIMES

Chapter Section

...lunch at the sixth hour is to be maintained if the monks have work in the fields or if the summer heat is excessive, and it is up to the abbot to provide for this. And he is similarly to adjust and dispose everything so that souls may be saved and the brothers may perform their activities without any justifiable murmuring. (41:4-5)

Discussion

Here it is again; keep the monks happy, don't give them cause to grumble. The abbot is expected to make exceptions. 'A wise man changes his mind, a fool never.' Hard and fast rules can be burdensome and the person in charge must possess the wisdom and authority to make appropriate changes. Situations change and rules must change with them. There are times when we have to put up with things which appear difficult or unjust, for the good of the community. And there are times when this is not necessary. The person in charge is the one who is trusted to make the distinction.

Prayer

Lord, help us to understand
the things that we find difficult to do,
and if we cannot understand,
help us to do them in your strength.
Amen.

Chapter Section

Indeed, in all seasons the hour for dinner or for the meal is to be adjusted so that everything can be done while there is still light. (41:9)

Discussion

There is a lot behind what St. Benedict says about deceptively simple things. This is an example of how he is deeply aware and thoughtful about the details of the lives of those in his charge.

Here is a story from the Zen tradition. One day, a new disciple came to the Zen master Joshu, and said, "I have just entered the brotherhood and I am anxious to learn the first principle of Zen. Will you teach me?"

"Have you eaten your supper?" Joshu asked in reply,

"Yes, I have eaten." Said the disciple.

"Then wash your bowl." Said the master.

In a similar way, the secret of the Benedictine life is to do well what you have to do, and then the ordinary becomes extraordinary.

Prayer

God, help us to take a fresh look
at the ordinary things we are asked to do
as the routine of each day.
We ask you to help us do everything well
and with new interest.
Amen.

Challenge

Say the Lord's Prayer with extra care today. Make it as extraordinary as it is.

CHAPTER 42: SILENCE AFTER COMPLINE

Chapter Section

At all times silence is to be studiously kept by monks, especially during the hours of night. (42:1)

Discussion

We have spoken about silence during the day—remember the chapters about the dining room? Is it any quieter there now? Keep trying!

This chapter is about silence at the end of the day. Do you go to your bedroom and start playing CDs, switch on the TV or radio? Or do you give a thought to God and offer up your day to him in a short, quiet prayer? —Something like, 'Thanks for the good things that happened today, God. And I'm sorry for the slip-ups." Can you then give time to listen? If you give God just a little of your silence, who knows what God will put into it. We are told in I Kings 19:11-13 that God is not in the whirlwind, the earthquake, the fire, but in the gentle breeze: a still, small voice. So, don't blow him away with noise!

Prayer

Jesus, I thank you for this day which is over.
Thank you for all the good that has happened.
I am sorry for anything I did wrong,
and I am sorry if I upset or hurt anyone.
Protect me while I sleep
and help me live tomorrow in a way that will please you.
Amen.

CHAPTER 43: THOSE WHO ARRIVE LATE AT THE WORK OF GOD OR AT TABLE

Introduction

The 'Work of God' (Opus Dei) in monasteries and convents is the saying of the Divine Office, which consists largely of reciting the Psalms. There were times when all 150 Psalms were said every day, (usually, now, the practice is to say them over a four week cycle). The point is, that when the bell rings for prayer, the monks and nuns obeyed immediately. Nothing was and is as important as the work of God.

Chapter Section

At the hour for the Divine Office, as soon as the signal is heard, he is [immediately] to lay aside everything he is doing and hasten with all speed... Thus nothing is to be preferred to the Work of God. (43:1, 3)

Discussion

'Immediately' —how often do we ignore that word in order to finish what we are doing? How often are we late to arrive where we are supposed to be? How about next time someone says, 'Immediately!' or 'Now!' we do what they say? Who will be the more surprised? Remember, the monks were responding to a bell, and a bell does not have feeling or the authority to punish. So, hurry up and avoid that tardy mark. This is a good chapter to remember for when there is a fire drill.

Prayer

God, we thank you for your patience,
make us aware that we need to respond to your call.
Give us a willing spirit towards you
and towards the needs of others.
Amen.

Chapter Section

If at table someone has not arrived before the verse, so that all may together say the verse, pray and sit down at the table... (43:13)

Discussion

At your school it may be impossible for everyone to sit down and eat together in the dining area. But we are able to sit together and pray and eat and drink at Mass and Holy Communion. If we consider Christ as the center of our school, and if we know that Christ is present in the Mass, then we have a golden opportunity to be at Christ's table together. Go to Mass. Don't be deterred by the idea that it is boring—it is not supposed to be hilarious entertainment. The Mass is where God's Son gives himself to us. Nothing is more important than being present to receive Christ.

Prayer

Jesus, you give us yourself in Holy Communion.
Why are we not there to receive you?
Forgive us when we have left a gap at your holy table.
Thank you for loving us.
Thank you for dying for us.
Renew our enthusiasm for the Mass.
Amen.

CHAPTER 44: THE EXCOMMUNICATED

Introduction

This chapter is for monks who committed faults to do with the Work of God, being late for chapel, or meals, and so on. In our context, we can think of excommunication as exclusion from class rather than exclusion from school.

Chapter Section

...he is to lie face down, prone on the ground at the feet of all as they leave the oratory; and he is to do this until the abbot judges that satisfaction has been made. (44:2, 3)

Discussion

The interruption of a class by a student is very annoying for the teacher, not to mention other students. It breaks the train of thought and stops others working, draws attention away from the group and onto an individual, and is, of course, selfish. Despite all this, it is not a good idea for the teacher to make the wrongdoer lie on the floor by the door! Teachers have to be very judicious and calm in dealing with those who interrupt the rhythm of learning and upset the carefully worked-out lesson plan. 'In quietness and in trust shall be your strength' [ISAIAH 30:15].

Prayers

God, you created us as individuals
but there are times when we need to be part of a group.
Help us to listen and learn in class
and not to distract others or ourselves.
Amen.

•

We pray for our teachers.
We thank you for their skill and knowledge.
We thank you for the care they spend in preparation
and correcting our work.
Amen.

Chapter Section

Those who for lesser faults are excommunicated only from the table are to make satisfaction in the oratory until the abbot gives the order: they do this until he gives his blessing and says: "It is enough." (44:9-10)

Discussion

It is interesting that, according to the Rule, when someone does wrong he is to go to the chapel to face God and ask his forgiveness. Perhaps in the quiet of the chapel and in the face of Christ, even the hardest of villains may think about their actions! Notice that when everything is put right, the wrongdoer is given a blessing. God does not bear grudges, nor should we.

Prayer

God, you are a just judge;
Jesus, you are a gentle friend.
Why do we let you down so often?
It is amazing that you forgive us always.
Make us want to try harder to please you.
Thank you.
Amen.

CHAPTER 45: FAULTS IN THE ORATORY

Introduction

In this short chapter Benedict is very clear about lack of concentration in saying the Psalms, making responses and reading in services. He adds that young people should be whipped for any fault in this regard!

Chapter Section

If anyone makes a mistake while reciting a psalm, responsory, antiphon or lesson, and does not make satisfaction, he is to be subjected to punishment. Children, however, are to be whipped for such faults. (45:1, 3)

Discussion

This is very harsh on children. Next time you are corrected for not doing your best or for not paying attention, be thankful that you are not living in the sixth century! But the passage illustrates how much importance St. Benedict places on concentration in services: reading and listening with reverence and care. How else are we going to know what God is saying to us? How often do we forget the response to the psalm?

In Benedict's time, it was common for children to be placed in monasteries for their education. Some of them would eventually become monks or nuns. The children as well as the adults were expected to give their full attention to the services.

Prayer

Lord, forgive us for not being attentive during prayers.
We all expect to be listened to when we speak.
How can we not be respectful
to someone who loves us so much?
Amen.

CHAPTER 46: FAULTS IN OTHER MATTERS

Introduction

We seem to be preoccupied by faults at the moment, but, let's face it, they happen all the time. We need all the direction we can get, and we should acknowledge it.

Chapter Section

If someone while laboring at any kind of work, whether in the kitchen, in the cellar, while serving, in the bakery, in the garden, at any craft or in any place, commits any fault... (46:1)

Discussion

This tells us that mistakes happen everywhere. That is not the important point. When mistakes happen, someone is responsible. There are no Mr. or Mrs. Nobodies in monasteries or in schools! Facing up to our mistakes is called 'accountability.' If you made a mistake, you know how it happened, you can account for it. Now, what are you going to do with this information?

This could be a good opportunity for you to silently reflect on what you know about yourself. Ask yourself, what do I do with what I know when the information is good? What do I do when it is not so good?

Prayer

God, I have just been thinking about myself.
You know what I am thinking.
You know what I admit and what I hide.
Help me always to be honest with myself and you,
for your love is greater than anything I have done wrong.
Thank you, God.
Amen.

Chapter Section

If someone breaks or loses something, or fails in any way whatever; and if he does not immediately go before the abbot or the community and of his own accord make satisfaction... he is to be subjected to more severe correction. (46:2-4)

Discussion

This section makes clear that when we do something wrong we cannot dismiss it with, "It doesn't matter, I've seen others do it, it's not important." Everything we do *is* important because it affects not only ourselves but also the community. No-one lives and works in isolation. What you do is important, whether right or wrong. And we all know the difference.

Prayer

God the Creator, they say that even when
a butterfly moves its wings,
it affects everything around it.
How much more do we affect
as we walk, talk, work and live in this community?
Help each one of us to realize how much
we influence each other,
and help us to be considerate.
Amen.

Chapter Section

If, however, the cause of the sin is hidden in the soul, he is to reveal it only to the abbot or to spiritual seniors who know how to heal both their own wounds and those of others without making them public. (46:5,6)

Discussion

St. Benedict is always very understanding, especially in the tough situations. Things that bother us are best shared. First we admit our difficulty to ourselves then we decide whom we should tell. It should be someone in authority who will help us. Preserving confidentiality is very important, that is, when you give someone your secret, they have to be trusted to keep it or to pass it on to someone equally trustworthy if they cannot deal with it to your satisfaction.

This is an opportunity to talk about the work of the school chaplaincy, if one is established at your school, and of the Sacrament of Reconciliation. One of the functions of priests is to hear confession and give absolution.

Prayer

Jesus, we ask for courage
to face up to things in our lives that need resolving.
Help us to find someone understanding to hear us,
someone who can give us special attention.
Amen.

Food for thought

Notice that St. Benedict uses the word 'heal.' Punishment is for healing, not to crush or humiliate. In the case of children, infuriating behavior may have a cause that takes much time and patience to understand.

CHAPTER 47: ANNOUNCING THE HOURS FOR THE WORK OF GOD

Introduction

Opus Dei, the Work of God, Prayer. There is nothing more important than prayer in a community. Prayer holds it together and gives it life and meaning. When time is not given to prayer, the community disintegrates.

Chapter Section

Announcing the hour for the Work of God day and night is the abbot's responsibility, whether he gives the signal himself or assigns this responsibility to a conscientious brother; so that all things may be completed at the appropriate time. (47:1)

Discussion

Prayer is so important that every day we are to be reminded by a senior person that it is to be done! People are very busy, we hear this all the time. If only we were busy praying! I once visited a school in Chile and was speaking with a head teacher in her office when the bell sounded for prayer. She asked me to join her and we went to the chapel where many of the students and staff had gathered to pray before they went to their lunch. How many of us think a routine like that would be appropriate?

There is an ancient monastic practice called *Lectio Divina*—Sacred Reading, which is a means whereby prayer is brought to the heart of a community. More about this important practice follows at the end of this book.

Prayer

God, we do not pray enough.
Help us to rethink the time we spend with you.
It is strange to think that you can answer all questions
and yet we are not interested in getting closer to you.
Amen.

CHAPTER 48: DAILY MANUAL LABOR

Introduction

In the Rule of St. Benedict Prayer and Work are two sides of the same coin. There is a balance, just as there has to be a balance in our lives between study and leisure.

Chapter Section

Idleness is the enemy of the soul; and therefore the brothers should be occupied at certain times in manual labor, and at certain other hours in sacred reading. (48:1)

Discussion

It would not be good to pray all day, to work all day, to study or to play all day. We need to vary our activities if we are to lead a balanced life. In school our timetable does that, except that it does not usually allow much time for prayer, so we have to fit that time in ourselves. Monks and nuns have bells to tell them when to pray. Schools have bells or buzzers to tell people when it is time to change lessons. But why do you think the prayer bell is missing?

Prayer

Jesus, you began your working life as a carpenter.
You continued your short life as a healer and teacher.
But you never forgot God.
Help us in our busy day to turn to God, Our Father,
in prayer.
Amen.

Chapter Section

...they are to labor at whatever is necessary from the first to about the fourth hour. From the fourth to the sixth they are to devote themselves to reading...after the table they are to rest...or read (in silence). None [prayer] is to be performed...in the eighth hour; then they are again to work until Vespers. ...Yet everything is to be done with proper measure on account of the fainthearted. (48:3-6, 9)

Discussion

This is an abbreviation of what St. Benedict proposes for the routine of a monastery during summertime. Though he is detailed, he is also flexible. The 'first hour' may be thought of as six o'clock in the morning (though that was not hard and fast in the days before clocks). Notice that Benedict includes plenty of time for reading (Lectio) during the working day. Then the final sentence about moderation reminds us to be balanced in all we do. For us, there should be a balance between homework and sports, chores and parties, and so on. We should not go over the top in anything.

Prayer

Jesus, sometimes we go over the top
and get things out of balance.
Help us to maintain a sense of balance in our lives,
remembering the things we have to do
as well as the things we want to do.
Amen.

Chapter Section

Above all, one or two seniors should be deputed to make the rounds of the monastery at the hours when the brothers are devoted to reading, and they are to see that there is not any brother giving in to idleness or idle story-telling, and does not apply himself to his reading: he is thus not only useless to himself but a distraction to others. If one is found (may it not happen!) he is to be corrected once and then a second time and if he does not amend, he is to be subjected to the chastisement of the Rule... (48:17-21)

Discussion

This should ring a bell. What happens if you are left to work on your own? People start talking and distracting others and everyone gets behind in their work. Fifteen hundred years ago St. Benedict had the same problem with his monks. Work is important, talking is important, having a laugh is very important, but each has to be done at the right time. We all know what the right time is for each activity. Let us try today to do everything at the right time and in the right place. If we did, we could all have a great day!

Prayer

God, there is a time and a place for everything.
Please help us today to do things right.
Thank you, God.
Amen.

Chapter Section

Brothers who are sick or weak are to be assigned such work or crafts that they will not be idle, and yet will not be oppressed by heavy labor and so driven away. Such infirmities are to be taken into consideration by the abbot. (48:24, 25)

Discussion

Here is a lesson in the value of every member of the community. Do we value our impaired students for the example they set us? Do we value the supervisors who look after us during lunch breaks? Do we value our bus drivers, our cleaners and janitors? If we take anyone for granted, we are devaluing someone whom God loves enough to die for. If we look for the Christ instead of the faults in each other, we can transform our school overnight.

Prayer

Jesus, you died for the person I don't like.
You died for the person who is impaired.
You died for the person who cleans up after us.
Jesus, we do not have the right to treat your friends
in any other way but as our friends.
Forgive us when we fail,
transform our community and ourselves.
Amen.

Challenge

Find ways to show people how you respect them: we are all God's children and each is deserving of the same respect. Respect things too: desks, chairs, books, equipment, as though they are special possessions. St. Benedict says that everything we are given for our benefit should be treated with the care that we have for the sacred vessels we use at Mass.

CHAPTER 49: THE OBSERVANCE OF LENT

Introduction

If we were perfect Christians, we would not need Lent. But this is the time we are given to concentrate on how to live the Christian life. It is a time for increased personal and community effort and it may help that as a class you support each other's personal pledges. Most importantly, don't abandon your pledge if something goes wrong, simply start again.

Chapter Section

Although at all times the life of a monk should be a Lenten observance, yet since few have the strength for this we encourage all during these days of Lent to keep themselves in all purity of life. (49:1,2)

Discussion

Lent is a time for getting rid of the clutter that has accumulated and blocked out God. Imagine a closet so full of stuff that you no longer know what is in there. Now is the time to sort everything out and decide what you no longer need. Perhaps it is God who has been pushed to the back of the closet.

Once there was a Zen master who had a visitor enquiring about Zen. Instead of listening, the visitor kept talking about himself. The master served tea and poured it into his visitor's cup and when it was full he kept pouring. The visitor pointed this out and the master said, "Just so. And like the cup you are filled with your own ideas. How can you expect me to give you the Zen unless you first empty your cup?"

Prayer

Lord, during this period of Lent,
let us be prepared to clear out some of the things
that block the path to you.
Help us to organize our lives and our time
so that we include you.
Amen.

Chapter Section

Therefore, during these days let us augment somewhat our usual quota of service through private prayers and abstinence from food and drink. (49:5)

Discussion

Do not only give up something for Lent, this can be a cop-out, do something extra. Of course you could always give up something you don't like—your least favorite vegetable perhaps! But what would be the point? When it comes to finding something to give up in order to discipline yourself, make it something that you would notice. How about television? Too difficult? But imagine the benefit of all the spare time you would have without television. Discipline, which comes from the word 'disciple,' helps us to develop when it is given by someone else. If it comes from ourselves it can develop us far more.

Prayer

Lord, we can make many excuses
about not doing things during Lent.
Help each one of us to quiet the rebel inside ourselves
and to do something positive this Lent.
Help us also to give up something we like
so that we discipline ourselves
instead of trying to satisfy our every whim.
Amen.

Chapter Section

...that is, by withholding from his body something of food, drink, sleep, excessive talking, ridiculing; and thus awaiting holy Easter with the joy of spiritual desire. (49:7)

Discussion

Well, that is simple enough to follow. What we have to decide is, do we want to follow it? If we think to ourselves that such abstinence is only for monks and nuns, then we are escaping our responsibilities as Christians. More and more I hear Benedictine monks and nuns saying that the Rule of St. Benedict was written for lay people too. That's us. If we want to be the people we know God created us to be, we need to make an effort.

Prayer

Help us, God Our Creator,
not to try to escape the fact
that we are to be the best that we can be.
And we need your help to be our best.
Thank you for giving us life.
Help us to fill our lives with what is good and true.
Amen.

Challenge

A pledge is something we think carefully about before committing to it. For Lent it may help us to think about our pledges, then write them down and place them in a box in chapel. This could be done at a special service to emphasize the importance of our intentions.

During Lent I will try to do:
- Something for God.........
- Something for others.........
- Something to improve myself.........
- Signature.........

CHAPTER 50:
BEING AWAY FROM THE COMMUNITY

Introduction

An old eastern saying says, 'Necessity changes a course but never a goal.' I suppose we can use a pun here to explain this saying and this chapter: a soccer player can be signed to another team, but the object of his job is to score goals whichever team he belongs to.

Chapter Section

Brothers who work some distance away and are not able to come at the proper hour to the oratory...should perform the Work of God there where they are...Similarly those sent on a journey should not allow the appointed hours to pass them by...thus not neglecting to offer their quota of service. (50:1-4)

Discussion

In earlier chpters St. Benedict has given clear directions about work and prayer and the times for doing them. But the ever-understanding Benedict says that being away from school is not an excuse for being lazy and skipping your work. If you have to go on vacation during school time, for instance, make sure you ask how best you can keep up with the class while you are away. Remember that when you are away from the school, the community is incomplete. You are important! Remember also to pray for the ones still hard at work.

Prayer

Jesus, there were times when
you went away from your disciples.
Help us to remember our responsibility to work
if we have to go away from school for any reason.
Help us to remember that each of us is
an important member of this community.
Amen.

CHAPTER 51:
BROTHERS WHO ARE NOT GOING FAR AWAY

Chapter Section

A brother who is sent out for some reason and expects to return that same day to the monastery, may not presume to eat outside, even if someone asks him to, unless he has been given permission by his abbot. If he acts otherwise he is to be excommunicated. (51:1-3)

Discussion

This chapter may seem harsh, but it is telling us that whether we are actually in our community or away for some reason, we are still members. Anything we do will reflect on our school. Many of us wear uniforms that identify us, but it is not for that reason that we are to be on our best behavior. It is because we belong somewhere and are, or should be, proud of where we belong. We should not want to do anything that will bring down our reputation or that of our school. As Christians, we cannot opt out of our community when we have opted in! Our Christian life does not start with Baptism and end with Confirmation. It is for life.

Prayer

God, at Baptism, we became members of your family.
You call us your children:
we are brothers and sisters of Jesus.
Why do we forget our Christian family ties?
Help us to look again at ways of coming close to you,
and of allowing you into our lives.
Amen.

CHAPTER 52:
THE ORATORY OF THE MONASTERY

Introduction

The oratory is a small church or chapel within a monastery.

Chapter Section

The oratory is to be what it is called, and nothing else should be done or kept there. (52:1)

Discussion

If there is a chapel in school, it is very important that it be kept as a sacred place. There are rooms and spaces for talking, studying, eating and writing. Chapel is not the place for any of these, it is a place dedicated to God and we give little enough space to God during the busy day, so this one place should be reserved for God. Sometimes a chapel is purpose-built, sometimes it may be a place adapted from a classroom or other room. It may be tempting to use God's space for other purposes. I remember a chapel that was once used to store luggage before a school trip. Not any more! Perhaps people think that because the chapel is empty it needs to be filled. Yes, it does, but with people praying. Sacred space. We do not talk to anyone in chapel except God.

Prayer

God, help us to see that a space set aside for you
is holy ground.
Give us an understanding and sense
of your presence in our lives and in our chapel
and in any space set aside for you.
Amen.

Chapter Section

When the Work of God is finished, all should go out in complete silence and with reverence for God, so that a brother who wishes to pray by himself will not be impeded by another's insensitivity. (52:2)

Discussion

Having called the chapel 'holy ground,' there should be such reverence that no one will want to spoil the peace and silence. However, if you do not recognize that this is holy ground you may not see the need to keep the silence. If the chapel is treated as a classroom where notebooks are taken and notices are given out, then it becomes a classroom. Rather, we should keep the silence, sit still and listen, create the sacred space so that the voice of God can be heard.

Prayer

God, I come into your real presence
and stand on holy ground.
I come to listen and to give you some time and space
in my life today.
Amen.

Challenge

Stay behind on your own after everyone has left the chapel and say the prayer above. Be still in God's presence and be assured that God is pleased you have stayed.

CHAPTER 53: THE RECEPTION OF GUESTS

Introduction

This is one of the most important chapters of the Rule. It is simple to read and to understand but it is perhaps the most difficult to carry out. However, if *everyone* in the community acts upon it, there will be dramatic effects both on the community and on its reputation. If it is ignored, the effects can be disastrous. Remember that bad news travels faster than good. Upsetting a visitor can cause great damage.

Chapter Section

All guests who present themselves are to be received as Christ, for He will say: I was a stranger and you took me in [MATTHEW. 25:35]. And to everyone fitting honor is to be shown... (53:1,2)

Discussion

As a school, perhaps even under the patronage of St. Benedict, we cannot claim that since our school is not a monastery this does not apply to us. Benedict backs up his Rule with scripture, so it is Jesus who is telling us how to receive guests. Jesus also said, "...As you did it to one of these the least of my brethren, you did it to me" [MATTHEW. 25:40]. Treat everyone as Christ, not only if you like them, or if the visitor happens to be the bishop or someone famous. You are to regard everyone who presents themselves as you would Christ, and not treat them rudely or without giving them proper attention.

Prayer

God Our Creator, you made us in your own image
yet sometimes we treat each other badly.
Help us to look for the Christ in each other,
and to speak and to act accordingly.
Give us the patience to try this today.
Amen.

Chapter Section

When, therefore, a guest is announced, he is to be met by the superior and the brothers with every ceremony of love: thus, first they are to pray together and thus be united to one another in peace. (53: 3,4)

Discussion

Just a minute. Such an effusive welcome may send many visitors rushing out the door! And then there are those unfortunate security measures that have to be carried out, with visitors having to check in and get a name tag. But we can still welcome guests in the spirit of St. Benedict, and apologize for our treating them like parcels at a post office. Perhaps their name tag could read, 'Today [date] we welcome [—] as our guest in the name of Christ. PAX.' Pax is the motto of Benedictine communities, it means 'Peace.'

Prayer

In the name of Jesus,
we ask that St. Benedict be with us
as we welcome guests to our school.
Help us to be worthy of Christ's love.
Help us to make visitors feel that
they have come to a place where
Christ and his gospel are a living reality.
Amen.

Chapter Section

...all humility is to be shown to all arriving or departing guests...The superior is to break his fast for the sake of the guest...Water is to be poured on the hands of the guests by the abbot, and the feet of all guests are to be washed by the abbot and the whole community. (53:6-13)

Discussion

Christ is in each one of us. This chapter refers again to scripture, where the abbot performs the humbling washing of feet, as Christ did for his disciples. In our relations with each other are we as humble? Do we treat each other as Christ in what we say to each other? It would be helpful if we could humbly, quietly correct each other when we see someone being treated in an unchristian way. We all fail at some time or another, we all need help, so if nothing is ever said, how can we expect to improve our community?

Prayer

We may be made in your image, God,
but sometimes we are poor images.
We ask for your help as we correct each other
in a friendly way.
We ask this as a Christian community
because it will help us to reflect your values
and most of all, your love.
Amen.

Chapter Section

In the reception of the poor and pilgrims the greatest care and solicitude should be shown, because in them Christ is more especially received... (53:15)

Discussion

St. Benedict goes into far more detail in this chapter than, for instance, in the chapter on how to behave in chapel. It is an uncomfortable chapter because it asks us to face up to our Christian responsibilities to exercise humility and compassion rather than authority. Imagine what would happen if a poor tramp were to wander onto the school premises. Someone is summoned to escort him away. He tries to say, "I've visited Benedictine communities before and they always..." But he is told, "Sorry, chum, this is a school. Go away before we call the police!" I have been fortunate, no, privileged, to visit Benedictine communities at home and overseas, and the hospitality is wonderful. It makes you feel as though you have come home. Be very careful how you treat people. Politeness costs nothing.

Prayer

Jesus, help us to see you in the poor and the stranger.
Let us treat people as our brothers and sisters,
because if you are our brother, that is just who they are!
Amen.

Challenge

Every school has a mission statement. Here is just one. Examine yours again in the light of Chapter 53 and think of how demanding it is. But be encouraged to follow it.

CHRIST WILL BE AT THE CENTER OF THIS COMMUNITY, WHICH WE WILL BUILD UP IN LOVE. WE WILL WORK AND PLAY IN HARMONY, TREATING EACH OTHER WITH DIGNITY AND JUSTICE. WE WILL DEVELOP POTENTIAL TO THE FULL AND STRIVE FOR EXCELLENCE.

CHAPTER 54: LETTERS AND GIFTS

Chapter Section

For no reason is it permissible for a monk to receive from his parents or from any other person—not even the brethren—letters, blessed objects, or any little gifts of any kind; nor may he give them to others, without permission of the abbot. (54:1)

Discussion

This may seem a very strict and uncharitable chapter, but in the days of 'I want so I get', of accumulating as much as we can, we can learn much from it. Monks have no personal possessions and so they are free from feelings of possessiveness. Everything needed is provided by the monastery. This emphasizes how much we depend on God. Having many possessions, we start to think we do not depend on God. When I was in Chile I found poor people who were devoted to God and what little they had they were prepared to give to the church community. Their needs were great; their need of God was greater.

Prayer

God, sometimes we ask for things that we want
rather than the things we need.
We need you in our lives, we need to give you praise.
Help us to ask for the things that you want us to have.
Help us to be grateful
and to remember those who have little.
Amen.

Food for Thought

Think of all the things you have. What could you live without? What do you want at the moment, for your birthday, for Christmas? Why do you want these things? If you get all the things you want, will you have to throw out other things to make room for them? Who gave you the most precious thing you have?

CHAPTER 55: CLOTHING AND FOOTWEAR

Introduction

There are twenty-two sections in this chapter, which shows how much importance St. Benedict places on our taking care of whatever we have and how we should look to the needs of others. Much can be made of this chapter with regard to the care of school equipment as well as personal belongings.

Chapter Section

Clothing is to be given to the brothers according to the nature of the place where they live and according to the climate; for in cold regions more is required and in warm regions less. ...[Allow] a scapular for work and to cover the feet, stockings and shoes. (55:1,2,6)

Discussion

Is there nothing Benedict does not think about and deal with in his Rule? Always practical, he gives the most sensible reasons for catering to the needs of the monks in his charge. Perhaps we should think of this when it comes to wearing school uniform. All the items on the list have some purpose and we should bear this in mind before we try to bend the rules.

Prayer

We thank you, God, for those who make the rules
because they are made for good reasons,
even when we cannot see them.
Help us to keep the rules of this community,
to look beyond their inconvenience and to see their value.
Amen.

Chapter Section

Concerning the color or coarseness of all these things, the monks should not complain; rather, whatever can be easily obtained in the province where they live or can be bought cheaply, they should use. The abbot is to see to the measurements, so that these garments are not too short... (55:7, 8)

Discussion

Anyone who has been in charge of making sure uniforms are worn properly should cheer to hear this! The length and fit of uniform skirts may be unfashionable but they are less likely to require safety pins than many garments that find their way to school. And boys with sneakers or trainers glued to their feet during class: there is a reason for uniform dress shoes.

Prayer

God Our Creator, why, when you give us so much,
do we want more, or the best or the latest?
We ask that we be satisfied with what we have,
that we consider what is truly important,
and that we think about the difference between
needing and wanting.
Amen.

Food for Thought

Do I make unfair demands on those who buy things for me? Do I want the clothes with the latest logos? Why? The last time I had something bought for me, did someone have to go without?

Chapter Section

On receiving new clothes, the old should always be returned at once, to be stored in the wardrobe for the poor. (55:9)

Discussion

Judging by the number of thrift stores or charity shops, most of us dispose of clothing before its time, though at least we pass it on so that those less fortunate can benefit. Joan Chittister asks, "Why is the world full of gorgeous garbage while the poor lack the basics of life?" We must ask ourselves why we are getting rid of some article of clothing. Have we outgrown it, or have we simply become tired of it? Is it worn out or has it suddenly become unfashionable? And do we take care of our clothes? The Benedictines have a reputation for good stewardship, for keeping things mended and orderly. How was your bedroom when you left it this morning?

Prayer

Lord, we have so much, we want so much,
and we don't treat properly what we have.
Help us to care for the things we have been given
and for what the community provides.
Amen.

CHAPTER 56: THE ABBOT'S TABLE

Chapter Section

The table of the abbot should always be with guests and pilgrims. Whenever there are few guests it is within his power to invite any of the brothers he wishes. He is, however, always to leave one or two seniors with the brothers for the sake of discipline. (56:1-3)

Discussion

Once again, Benedict shows us the importance of the guest. Benedictine hospitality does not consist only of food and a place to stay, but spiritual needs are also met, with warmth and friendship. This is an example for us in welcoming our visitors.

But when it comes to being invited to the head table, it might make for jealousy of the sort that can destroy a community, so Benedict makes sure that not all the 'seniors' are at the abbot's table. Those in authority should always keep in mind the feelings of the community and steer it on a smooth course.

Prayers

May all who visit our community find a welcome
that befits Christ himself.
Amen.

•

Lord, help us to avoid being jealous.
Jealousy can destroy relationships.
We ask for guidance as we form and build relationships.
May they benefit the whole community.
Amen.

CHAPTER 57: ARTISANS

Chapter Section

If there are craftsmen in the monastery, they are to practice their crafts in all humility if the abbot permits it. (57:1)

Discussion

The word 'If' is surprising. There are always gifted people in a community, and schools are always hotbeds of budding talent. The responsibility of the school is to develop those gifts; the responsibility of the individual is to use his or her gift. The community certainly can lose out if people are shy or selfish with their special gifts. Read the Parable of the Talents in Luke 19:11-27. Then perhaps act out a short drama based on it.

Prayer

For all your gifts, we thank you, God.
Help each of us to develop the gifts and talents
that you have given us.
Help us to use them for your glory
and for the good of the community.
Amen.

Chapter Section

But if any one of them becomes conceited because of his knowledge of his craft, determining that he thus confers something on the monastery, he is to be taken from that craft and not permitted to exercise it again, unless having humbled himself, the abbot orders him back to it. (57:2,3)

Discussion

The opposite of being shy and not using your gift is showing-off, being big-headed and conceited. Then, no matter how great your gift, it has brought out the worst and it has to be dealt with. Hopefully, in school we do not encourage those who are talented to the detriment of others in the community, rather we help people acquire a healthy attitude towards their gifts. We must guard against creating big-heads! Big hearts, yes, there can never be too many of those.

Prayer

Jesus, your gifts of preaching, healing and care for others
shine through the gospels.
None of your gifts was used in the wrong spirit.
We ask that you help us to share our gifts in the right way,
and always to be thankful for them.
Amen.

CHAPTER 58: RECEIVING NEW MEMBERS

Chapter Section

One newly arriving to this way of life is not to be granted an easy entrance; rather, as the apostle says, 'Test the spirits, whether they are from God.' [I JOHN 4:1] Therefore if the one who comes perseveres in knocking and appears to patiently endure injuries done him... for four or five days and if he still persists in his petition, entrance is to be granted... (58:1-4)

Discussion

Life in a monastic community is not a running away from the world or a soft-option, so care has to be taken that people enter for the right reason. Religious schools are slightly different. Parents are asked why they choose such a school, and there are reasons other than convenience or good discipline. The best reason is that this is a school of faith. We who are involved in Catholic education should be in no doubt that the faith is a priority, vital to the daily life of the school. Morning prayers are not optional, assemblies are religious rather than administrative, the Mass is a community celebration not an obligatory dirge. Those who organize worship and praise in the school have an important responsibility.

Prayer

God, sometimes we find ourselves coming to school
only for our secular education.
Help each one of us realize that you are part of our life
and witness in this school.
We ask for the prayers of [Our Patron]
to guide us as we pray, work and study.
Amen.

Chapter Section

The one being received is to make in the oratory before all a promise of stability, faithfulness to the way of life and obedience. (58:17)

Discussion

Although we are not entering a religious congregation, we are in a community, and we have a loyalty to promote it in any way that we can as a school with good values. We have a duty to keep the rules as set down in the school documents. We also have a duty to obey those in authority at whatever level. Those in authority have the duty to be wise and fair. We are accountable to each other. The Rule of St. Benedict may demand a complete change in the way we live! As we have seen before, it is not simply for reading or study, It is for LIVING. When the Rule is lived it changes both religious and lay communities.

Prayer

God the Creator,
Jesus the Redeemer,
Holy Spirit the Sanctifier,
help us to live this Rule for your glory
and for the good of our community.
Amen.

CHAPTER 59:
OFFERING NOBLE AND POOR CHILDREN

Introduction

Offering children to a monastery was customary in the days of St. Benedict. It was believed that the family and the child would be assured of salvation. Until the Council of Trent, the practice was commonplace. After the sixteenth century, only adults could be admitted to religious profession. Parents did not put children in monasteries to get rid of them!

Chapter Section

If a member of the nobility offers his son to God in the monastery and if the child is of tender years, his parents are to make the petition...and, together with the offerings they are to wrap that petition and the hand of the child in the altar-cloth, and so offer him. (59:1, 2)

Discussion

This may seem extreme behavior, but it was what people were prepared to do to show their devotion and to be assured of salvation. What are we prepared to give at the Offertory, at the Presentation of Gifts? Are we prepared to give ourselves? We give, not because we want to buy salvation, but because we have the opportunity to give a little back to God from whom we receive everything.

Prayer

God, at the Offertory we are used to offering you
the bread and the wine and the collection of money.
Help us to see that the best we can offer
is the gift of ourselves
in your service and the service of others.
Amen.

Chapter Section

With regard to his property, in that same petition, they are to promise under oath that they will never, either directly, through an intermediary, or in any other way give him anything or the means of having anything... they are [instead] to make a donation to the monastery... that no sort of expectation will remain by which the child might be deceived and perish, which experience has taught us may happen. (59:3, 5-6)

Discussion

It is difficult for the rich not to use their money to influence others. St. Benedict makes it clear that the child is not to have any special allowance because his family is wealthy. The donation is to be made to the monastery, not the child. If we do have parents who can afford to give large amounts of money, it is wiser that the donation be made to some school project or fund rather than let their child spend it frivolously.

Prayer

Help us, God, never to use what we have
to gain favor with others,
for all we have comes from you.
Amen.

Chapter Section

Those who are poorer are to do the same. But those who have nothing whatever are to simply make the petition and offer their son along with the offerings before witnesses. (59:7-8)

Discussion

What money do you have to offer? None? Come on in, you are just as welcome! There is no discrimination here. St. Benedict accepts everyone who comes in the right spirit. The right spirit has nothing to do with wealth. So, in a school community there should be no discrimination of any kind. We are all children of God, brothers and sisters of Jesus, who was born in a stable, became a refugee, and after a life spent on the move was hung on a cross as a common criminal. Who are we to gloat over our possessions or bemoan what we do not have? We can only look at our generous God and his Son, Jesus, and say, Thank you! And can we say our prayer wholeheartedly?

Prayer

All that I am,
all that I do,
all that I ever have
I offer now to you.
Amen.

CHAPTER 60: PRIESTS WHO WISH TO LIVE IN THE MONASTERY

Introduction

St. Benedict was not a priest. He wanted to remain a hermit but was asked to be the abbot of a group of monks. Occasionally, secular priests joined the community. Benedict makes it clear that they were not to be given special privileges.

Chapter Section

If anyone ordained to the priesthood asks to be received into the monastery, assent should not be granted him too quickly. But if he persists in this request, he must know that he will have to keep all the discipline of the Rule... Nevertheless, it is permitted him to stand in the next place after the abbot, to give the blessing, and to celebrate Mass... He is to regard as his place that which corresponds to his time of entry in the monastery. (60:1-2, 4, 7)

Discussion

This chapter is about joining a community after being part of another system. Priests were learned and respected outside the monastery. On entering their new life they had to be prepared to let go of their status. It is difficult for anyone to enter an established community. We must welcome newcomers and help them to settle.

Prayer

God, we thank you for our community.
Help us to be attentive to those who join today.
Give us open and generous hearts
so that they may feel you are at the center
of our lives and our work in this place.
Amen.

Food for Thought

Do you have experience of joining a new school in mid-term? How did you deal with the situation?

CHAPTER 61:
HOW VISITING MONKS ARE RECEIVED

Chapter Section

If a pilgrim-monk arrives from distant provinces and wishes to stay as a guest in the monastery... [and] if he reasonably and with humble charity criticizes or suggests something, the abbot should prudently consider whether the Lord may not have sent him for this very reason. (61:1, 4)

Discussion

This is quite difficult to put into practice, but St. Benedict usually gives wise advice. You have a very good set-up, and along comes someone from another organization and makes some very good suggestions. Do you tell them to mind their own business? Do you wait until they have gone and then ignore their suggestions? Or do you think things through and try to adopt the ideas? We do not like to be challenged as it often means making uncomfortable changes. But criticism can be an opportunity for growth. On the other hand, too much criticism or unconstructive criticism can be corrosive and should not be tolerated

Prayer

Jesus, sometimes criticism is useful
though it may be hard to accept.
Sometimes criticism is harmful,
especially when we add to it unnecessarily.
Help us to see good in others,
and if we need to criticize, let us do it lovingly,
for the best reasons and in the gentlest manner.
Amen.

CHAPTER 62:
THE PRIESTS OF THE MONASTERY

Introduction

Working in school communities, we tend to forget what unusual places they are, with their hectic pace and special jargon. Some priests and lay people from outside express that they feel overwhelmed in such a situation, this is natural, and we must pay special attention to them to avoid misunderstandings. (See Chapter 53).

Chapter Section

If any abbot requests to have a priest or deacon ordained for himself, he should choose from among his own, one who is worthy to function as a priest. The one who is ordained is to be cautious of arrogance and pride and not presume to do anything he has not been commanded by the abbot... His priesthood should not cause him to forget the obedience and discipline of the Rule... Should he presume to do otherwise he will be judged not a priest but a rebel... and if he does not amend... he is to be expelled from the monastery. (62:1-4, 8-10)

Discussion

If you are in the community, you keep the Rule. Sadly, some people have the idea that priests are a higher form of Christian. This has never been the case. We are here to be what God asks: teacher, student, janitor, librarian, nurse. We must never allow what we do to obscure that we are all children of God, individuals who make up a community, and the community revolves around God at the center.

Prayer

We give thanks, Lord, for the priests
who come to celebrate the sacraments for us.
May our community always make them welcome,
for we are asked to treat everyone as Christ.
Amen.

CHAPTER 63: RANK IN THE COMMUNITY

Chapter Section

They are to keep their rank in the monastery which the time of their entry and the merit of their lives determines... The juniors, therefore are to honor their elders, and the elders love the younger. ...The abbot, since he is believed to represent Christ, is to be called 'Lord' and 'Abbot;' ...Let him ponder this, and behave in such a way as to be worthy of such honor. (63:1,10, 13, 14)

Discussion

There should be mutual respect, the younger for the older and the older for the younger. The older person, because of his experience, has the greater responsibility to show an example to the younger. We are always ready to correct younger people but have we always shown them the best example? Do we say, "Shut up! Don't speak to me like that! How dare you behave like that?" Respect, responsibility and example are Benedictine traits. To shout down and humiliate another are not. As it says in Romans 12:10, 'Outdo one another in showing honor.'

Prayer

It is obvious that we should respect our elders,
but not so obvious that we should respect our juniors,
and not so easy.
Jesus, give all of us the grace
to be responsible to and for each other.
Amen.

Chapter Section

Outside, or wherever else they may be, small children and adolescents are to receive care and discipline until they reach the age of reason. (63:19)

Discussion

There is a caring feeling about this section. Controlling children just for the sake of it is not the idea. Rather, St. Benedict teaches us to respect the spark of God in everyone, the older people are to set an example for the younger.

Here is a Zen story for the class to discuss. —A wealthy Zen Master was invited to a banquet. But when he arrived at the hall he was not recognized because he had decided to wear beggar's rags, and was promptly turned away. He went home, changed into his finest ceremonial robe and returned to the banquet, where he was received with great respect and shown to the place of honor. The Master took off his marvelous robe and set it up on his chair and turning to leave said, "I presume it is my robe that you invited to this banquet, since you sent me away when I was wearing beggar's clothes!"

Prayer

We thank you, God, for creating each of us
in your own image.
You have not created us in our idea of your image!
We ask for the spirit of respect
in dealing with each other.
Amen.

CHAPTER 64: APPOINTING AN ABBOT

Introduction

Staff and students of a school do not elect their leader, though they may have representatives in the selection committee. St. Benedict tells us what we should look for in a leader: someone who is good and wise and who brings out the best in us. Benedictine spirituality opts for ideals, even at those times when pragmatic management seems more important than vision.

Chapter Section

It is for the merit of his life and wisdom of his teaching that the one appointed should be chosen, even if he comes last in community rank. (64:2)

Discussion

We may not have the opportunity to choose an abbot or a head teacher, but we may have to choose some other person to lead or represent us. Goodness is the main quality we should look out for. Do not be tempted to choose the best speaker, the toughest, the biggest, the loudest, or –God forbid– the one who has twisted your arm! Trust is also very important, without mutual trust a leader can do little.

Prayer

We pray for those who have been chosen to lead.
We pray especially for [Name].
We pray for all those in authority
that they may lead with goodness and wisdom,
seeking always the good of the community.
Amen.

Chapter Section

But even if it were the entire community that acted together in electing a person (and may this never happen!) who consented to their vices... (64:3)

Discussion

There should be no fixing, no cheating, no 'jobs for the boys,' no politics. The work of anyone who is chosen in such a way is doomed from the start. Anyone who takes a place of authority for their own good or at the bidding of someone outside the community is not worthy of the position, and cannot command the respect of the community.

Prayer

Guard us, O God, from those who would place
their own interests before those of the community.
May we always be honest and fair
in our dealings with each other.
Amen.

Chapter Section

The one appointed must know how much more fitting it is to provide for others than to preside over them. He is to hate vices and love the brothers. But in correcting them he is to act prudently and avoid extremes, lest in trying too ardently to scrape off the rust, he breaks the vessel: his own frailty he must always keep before his eyes, recalling that 'the bruised reed is not to be broken' [ISAIAH 42:3]. And he should strive to be loved rather than feared. (64: 8, 11, 12, 13, 15)

Discussion

In case we are ever called to lead, at whatever level, we need to be aware of these wise words and adopt them. Then we can be confident that we will lead in a good and wise way, we will be trustworthy and respected.

Prayer

God, we remember before you,
all those who have to make decisions today.
May they make them with your guidance
and with the good of the community
in their minds and hearts.
Amen.

Chapter Section

[The abbot] is not to be turbulent anxious, nor excessive and obstinate, nor jealous and prone to suspicion; for otherwise he will never be at rest. In his commands he is to be farsighted and considerate... reflecting on the discretion of holy Jacob, who said: 'If I drive my flocks too hard, they will all die in one day' [GENESIS 33:13]. And in particular he is to keep this Rule in every way. (64:16-18, 20)

Discussion

A person who is never at rest has no time for people. The abbot must have time for his community, after all, we spend time with whom or what we care about. And there are to be no special favors for those in charge. If you are a classroom monitor, entrusted with the class key, this does not mean you can hold wild parties there with your friends when school is out. It might make you popular with a few, but others will lose respect for you.

Prayers

Lord, we pray for this community,
that it may be effectively run
and carefully and lovingly administered.
We pray that you will be at the community's center,
and in the hearts and minds of those
who hold authority.
Amen.

•

We pray for our Head Teachers.
May they be guided by you, God, in all decisions.
Bless them with your wisdom and strength.
Amen.

Food for Thought

If you were chosen to lead this community, what would you change, and why? If you were a Principal or Head Teacher what do you think would give you the most cause for worry?

CHAPTER 65: THE PRIOR OF THE MONASTERY

Introduction

The prior is the second-in-command of the monastery, and in Benedictine communities is chosen by the abbot to take charge in his absence.

Chapter Section

This prior is to perform with reverence what the abbot demands of him, doing nothing contrary to the abbot's will or organization; for the more he is elevated above the rest, the more solicitously he ought to observe the precepts of the Rule. (65:16, 17)

Discussion

Being second-in-command is difficult: you are nearly in charge, but not quite! Loyalty is the name of the game, you stick by what your boss says and defend his or her decisions. If you do otherwise, you cause confusion and disharmony in your community. Of course if the boss is away, then it is up to you to make decisions, and that is the way it should be.

Prayer

Lord, we pray for Deputy-Heads and Vice-Principals,
that they may carry out their duties with loyalty
and strive for harmony in this community
at all times.
Amen.

CHAPTER 66: THE MONASTERY PORTERS

Introduction

The monastery porter is not the one who carries the bags, but the one who waits to answer the door or, today, the telephone. Writing about the duties of the porter immediately after those of the abbot and the prior perhaps indicates the importance St. Benedict gave to this position.

Chapter Section

At the door of the monastery should be placed a wise old man who knows how to take a message and give one, and whose maturity keeps him from wandering. This porter ought to have his room near the door, so that those who arrive will always find someone present to take their message. (66:1, 2)

Discussion

It is hard to believe that something so practical today was written fifteen hundred years ago. It is no good being appointed to answer the door if you have a tendency to wander off! This chapter echoes the important previous material about receiving guests, and in this context Chapter 53 is worth revisiting.

Prayer

We pray for those who receive our visitors.
May they always receive them as Christ.
May those who visit feel welcomed
and that they have come to a Christ-centered place.
Amen.

Chapter Section

As soon as anyone knocks or a poor person calls out, the porter should respond, "Thanks be to God!" or, "Please give your blessing." And with all the gentleness of the fear of God, he is to respond quickly with the fervor of love. If the porter requires help, a younger brother should be given to him. (66:3-5)

Discussion

Whether you are at the school reception or the door of your classroom, if it is your job to respond to everyone who knocks, it is also your privilege and joy! No one is to be considered a nuisance because every visitor is to be welcomed as Christ. Notice that St. Benedict has the porter ask for the blessing of all visitors—including poor people. When someone knocks at the door of a Benedictine community, they should never be told to go away. Sister Joan Chittister says, "Come in the middle of lunch, come in the middle of prayer, come and bother us with your blessing anytime..."

Prayer

Jesus, when we are given the privilege
of greeting someone,
of answering a knock at the door,
may we look for you in that guest.
May no one ever feel unwelcome
in our community.
Amen.

CHAPTER 67: BROTHERS SENT ON A JOURNEY

Chapter Section

Brothers sent on a journey are to commend themselves to the prayers of all the brothers and of the abbot; on returning, they request the prayers of all for their faults in case they have seen or heard anything evil on their journey... (67:1, 4)

Discussion

When away, we are ambassadors for our community. And the community is incomplete when any member is missing, for whatever reason. The idea that there may be problems when you are away suggests that in your community you are among friends where no one would hurt you or get you into trouble, but things could be different outside. There could be temptations and people trying to lead you astray. Benedict assumes that the community is a safe and friendly place, and so it should be, without fights or bullies. Let us build a community like this!

Prayer

Lord, we pray for those who are absent:
those who are ill at home or in hospital,
those who are on vacation,
and those who are suspended.
We remember all of them because without them
this community is incomplete.
Amen.

CHAPTER 68: IF AN IMPOSSIBLE TASK IS COMMANDED OF A BROTHER

Introduction

Once, over a period of three days, I was interviewed for the position of School Chaplain. After the second day I felt that something superhuman was required for me to land the job. I chanced upon this chapter in an old copy of the Holy Rule—my introduction to St. Benedict's work. It fit the occasion beautifully and, as it happens, I got the job.

Chapter Section

If a brother is commanded to do hard or impossible things, he should receive the order of his superior with all gentleness and obedience. But if he sees that the measure of his strength is exceeded by the weight of the burden, he is to explain the cause of his incapacity to his superior...But if the superior persists in his command, the junior must know that it is best for him; and out of love, confident of God's help, he is to obey. (68: 1-2,4-5)

Discussion

They key here is to trust in God's help. We often try to go it alone even though God's help is freely available. As the simple version of the Prayer of St. Benedict says, 'I'll do anything you ask, God, but just give me a hand!' If we brought God into the process, homework would not be a problem. Try it. But remember you must do your part, handing your books to God while you watch TV is not the way! In prayer we discover God's will for us.

Prayer

God, you know we live in a proud, arrogant society.
We want to be independent,
yet if we were to invite you into our lives
every area would be better.
I will move over my pride so that you can come in.
Amen

CHAPTER 69: NOT DEFENDING ANOTHER IN THE MONASTERY

Chapter Section

Every precaution must be taken that no one in the monastery presumes on any occasion to defend another monk or to act as his protector... If anyone transgresses this, he is to be severely punished. (69:1, 4)

Discussion

Leaping to someone's defence can seem very loyal, but it often leads to misunderstandings and involves others in situations which are not their business. Taking sides causes untold problems in school: he said, she said, they said, tempers raised, and before we know it there's a war on. People have to be left to deal with their own situations. As to your response, have you ever thought about trusting in God, inviting him in to the problem and 'listening with the ear of your heart?' There is no need to tell God all the details, he knows them already. God can sort out the problem. Try it!

Prayer

God, give us the courage and wisdom
to stand back from a problem
when we might complicate it.
We pray for those who have difficulties now.
Help them let you help them.
Amen.

CHAPTER 70: THAT THEY MAY NOT PRESUME TO STRIKE ONE ANOTHER

Chapter Section

...we decree that no one has the right to excommunicate or strike any of his brothers, unless he has received power to do so by the abbot. (70:2)

Discussion

One would hope that the abbot would never give permission to hit anyone—despite the fact that some of his monks might have been ex-robbers, soldiers and the like! Fighting to solve a problem is tempting, but the Rule says here that there is to be none. Fighting solves nothing either in the short or the long-term. I am sure that fighting of any sort makes God very sad, and wonder what sort of people he has created!

Prayer

God, we live in a violent world.
Pictures and reports of violence are all around us.
We pray that we will never be the cause of violence
to any of your children.
Help us to remember that we are your children
and brothers and sisters of Jesus
who came to bring peace to our world.
May we help to bring peace to any situation we can.
Amen.

CHAPTER 71: THAT THEY SHOULD OBEY ONE ANOTHER

Chapter Section

Not only is the blessing of obedience to be shown by all to the abbot; the brothers must also obey one another, knowing that by this path of obedience they go to God. Anyone who is found to be quarrelsome is to be corrected. (71:1-2, 5)

Discussion

Just after being told that we are not to stick up for one another and then that we are not to hit one another, we are told that we have to obey each other. And why not? If we listen to people rather than shout at them, if we build each other up instead of putting each other down, what a marvelous place we would have in which to live and work! Because we are human we make mistakes and harm our friends and our community. St. Benedict was human too. But his ideals came from God rather than the world. Difficult, but right.

Prayer

Lord, obedience is always difficult,
but obedience to each other
—that is going to take something special.
The something special is you at the center.
Help us to keep you in the center of our lives.
Amen.

Chapter Section

If a monk comes to believe that any superior is angered or perplexed about him, however trivially, he should immediately cast himself on the ground at his feet, remaining there until the turmoil is healed by the other's blessing. But if anyone is too haughty to do this... he must be expelled from the monastery. (71:7-9)

Discussion

Even if we take the idea of prostrating ourselves at someone else's feet as a metaphor, no doubt most people will think this is difficult, and so it is. But if we have upset someone then the sooner the apology is made and the hurt healed, the better. We have all known the ongoing feuds that lead nowhere. We all need to live and work together acknowledging that we are not perfect, that we are sinful, and that we depend on the forgiveness of God and each other if we are going to move on.

Prayer

Jesus, we have sinned against you and our neighbor
and we are no longer worthy
of being called your children.
But your love and forgiveness are freely given.
Help us to be generous in forgiving each other.
Amen.

Challenge

Is there anyone you need to see about asking their forgiveness? No, it is not easy, if it were, you would have done it earlier than this! Find that person today and tell them you are sorry.

CHAPTER 72:
THE ZEAL THAT MONKS OUGHT TO HAVE

Chapter Section

None should follow what he judges useful for himself, but rather what is better for another... preferring nothing whatever to Christ, and may he bring us all together to life everlasting. Amen. (72:7, 11-12)

Discussion

In this penultimate chapter, St. Benedict still keeps giving more and more to us. He reinforces that we must constantly pay attention to other people rather than to ourselves. And then there is the jewel: 'Prefer nothing to Christ.' If we could only take that to heart, not just read it or post it on a wall, we would not need any other maxim. We would be keen, zealous to do good for others rather than being selfish, and Christ would be at the center of our community.

Prayer

God Our Creator, let us allow you to mold us.
Make us keen to serve you and each other.
Make us eager to do good.
We ask for your Spirit
and the gifts we need to grow towards you
Amen.

CHAPTER 73: ALL OF JUST OBSERVANCE IS NOT CONTAINED IN THIS RULE

Chapter Section

We have written this Rule so that, by observing it... we may demonstrate that we have somewhat grasped honorable behavior and the beginnings of ascetical practice. But for those hastening to perfection, there are the teachings of the Holy Fathers, the observance of which leads one to the height of perfection. (73:1, 2)

Discussion

Just as we finish this Rule, St. Benedict downplays it, saying that practicing it gives us the way to behave so that we can make a beginning on ideal Christian life. Furthermore he tells us that if we want to achieve perfection, we should turn to the teachings of the early Church. In any event, this Rule has been used successfully by religious communities for fifteen hundred years, it changes people for the better. And it can change you and your community.

Prayer

Lord, we thank you for the Rule
of our Holy Father Benedict.
May it teach and inspire us throughout our lives.
Let us not be afraid to take on this challenge
which can change our lives
and the way in which we serve you and each other.
Amen.

Chapter Section

Whoever you are, therefore, hastening toward your heavenly homeland; fulfill with the help of Christ this little Rule for beginners we have written: and then at last you will arrive under God's protection at the loftier summits of doctrine and virtue we have spoken of above. Amen. (73:8-9)

Discussion

What do we do now? In true Benedictine fashion, we go back to the beginning and start again with the words of the Prologue. An elderly nun wrote to me once and said, "As one who has lived the Rule of Benedict for more than half my lifetime, I find it a fount of wisdom that never runs dry." They key word there is 'lived.' This is a practical, living, spiritual Rule. Now return to the Prologue and begin again with the words, 'Listen... and incline the ear of your heart.' You will find more each time you read the Rule and your community will benefit every day you live it. God bless you in the journey and may St. Benedict accompany you along the path. Let us pray, once more, the prayer attributed to him.

Prayer

We pray, Lord, that everything we do
may be prompted by your inspiration,
so that every prayer and work of ours
may begin from you
and be brought by you to completion.
Amen.

LECTIO DIVINA IN A SCHOOL COMMUNITY

People shall not live by bread alone, but by every word that proceeds from the mouth of God [MATTHEW 4:4].

This ancient method of reading the scriptures was practiced by St. Benedict himself and is mentioned in Chapter 47 of the Rule. It is still widely practiced by Benedictines today. Lectio has nothing to do with intellect, analysis or scholarship, in fact these may actually hamper Lectio in the early stages. It is appropriate that the Rule begins with the word 'Listen.' Lectio simply means listening to the Word of God as it is read slowly. So, I hear what God is saying to *me*. This does not mean that God is going to ask me to save the world, but that God has something to say to every individual who will 'Listen with the ear of the heart.'

St. John of the Cross summarizes the four phases of Lectio, alluding to words in the Gospel of St. Luke:

Seek in *Reading*
and you will find in *Meditation;*
knock in *Prayer*
and it will be opened to you in *Contemplation.*

If it is to open lines of communication between God and his children, beginning a school Lectio group is a great responsibility. The leader should be well prepared with thought and prayer. As an exercise, it may be a good idea to begin by using a secular poem. Make it fun, ask each student what line jumped out at them. Often there are a great variety of answers, thus demonstrating that words mean different things to different people. Once the students are used to the process, move onto something from scripture. Many of the Psalms have graphic words and imagery, and they make a good transition.

The Christian Bible is the world's most published book. Almost all Christian homes have a copy or two. Most other world religions can give us lessons in how to treat sacred scripture. How are Bibles handed-out in your school, and in what condition are they? Often they are neglected, and children have been conditioned to treat sacred scripture with disdain. This can be a hurdle to overcome for a leader starting the Lectio process, and he or she must find creative ways to inspire children with the idea that the Word of God is waiting for us to tap into for direction. Emphasizing that the Bible is directed at the *individual* will help. And it is to be read slowly. Each of us is to listen with our heart.

Two models for conducting a Lectio session follow. But first, in developing a technique for practicing Lectio Divina there are a number of things that should be done and a number that should be avoided. From the outset everyone in the group should be aware of them.

What To Do

• To represent the presence of the Light of Christ, have a lit candle or a cross as a focal-point.

• The meeting begins with a prayer to the Holy Spirit.

• Help each other to feel relaxed, sit quietly and open your Bibles at the selected text. If everyone has the same version and edition, a page number can be given, and this saves those less familiar with books, chapters and verses from being distracted.

• Unless someone else has prepared a specific text, the leader is to read. The text should be read well. (See chapter 38 of the Rule).

• Time should be given for reflection and then the text is read again slowly. There is a pause and then an opportunity for each to share what they hear in their heart, the *echo*.

• The echo is given in the first person: "The passage means this to me..." or, "God is showing me..." No one is required to make their comment. But as the group feels more at ease, more will.

• When everybody has had a chance to comment there should be a period of silence and then a closing prayer.

• Keep your Lectio group to under ten people. If more want to participate, another group should be formed. In Chile, where I found that 900 groups had been formed throughout the country over the past 25 years, groups of the same sex and similar ages were regarded as the most successful, since these allowed their members to be most comfortable.

• In order to achieve the simple discipline of Lectio without floundering, it is best that leaders have some experience of the process before forming a new group.

• Remember to arrange the next meeting!

What to Avoid

• Group Lectio is a time for intimate encounter with God. Make every effort to ensure our noisy, busy lives outside the group do not intrude.

• Do not allow comment on the 'echoes' that the participants express.

• Do not encourage participants to brag about their knowledge or to analyze a text exegetically.

• Guard against using the Bible as a fortune-teller. Remember the story of the person who opened his Bible at random to read, 'Judas went out and hanged himself.' He closed it quickly and then opened it to, 'Go and thou do likewise.' Beware!

Model of Lectio Sessions —A

Within the Daily Office (Midday Praise).

1. Introduction and references of chosen text(s).
2. Office proceeds until readings.
3. One to five readings are read slowly. One is usually the Gospel for the following Sunday.
4. Reflective silence.
5. Echoes. These are always made in the first person. They can be made as a prayer. There are no interruptions or comments from others.
6. Intercessions from the group.
7. Closing prayer.
8. Grace.

Model of Lectio Sessions —B

1. Introduction and references of chosen text(s).
2. Prayer to the Holy Spirit.
3. Prayer of St. Benedict:

> We pray, Lord, that everything we do
> may be prompted by your inspiration,
> so that every prayer and work of ours
> may begin from you
> and be brought by you to completion.

4. Readings,
5. Reflective Silence.
6. Echoes.
7. The Lord's Prayer.
8. Intercessions.
9. Grace.

SAINT BENEDICT PRAY FOR US

✙

PAX

Printed in the United Kingdom
by Lightning Source UK Ltd.
117737UKS00001BA/226-453